Armadillos and Yellow Lines

essays from *The Huffington Post*

Hoyt Hilsman

Preface

When *The Huffington Post* editors asked me to join as a contributor in the fall of 2008, I had a just finished a second unsuccessful campaign for Congress in California, but I still had lots to say about the politics and culture of our country. Unlike the other publications and media outlets that I had written for, *The Huffington Post* gave me the opportunity to write on whatever topic I chose and I quickly took advantage of the virtual soapbox. Since then, I have written over a hundred essays for *HuffPost*, on topics ranging from gun control to Brittney Spears, with a focus on American politics and culture.

I am an unabashed Democratic centrist, or more precisely center-left. I believe in an activist government to meet the needs of all the people, but I also believe that government should be effective and efficient, with as little waste of money and human resources as possible. While I have frequently taken the Right to task for their excesses during the Obama presidency, I have also been a critic of some of President Obama's policies and politics. And I am a big fan of bipartisanship and appropriate compromise, even with those with whom I vehemently disagree.

So all that puts me squarely in the middle of the road as a political and social commentator, which leads to an explanation of the title of this volume of essays – *Armadillos and Yellow Lines*. Those readers of political commentary will recognize this as a reframing of the Jim Hightower quote: "There's nothing in the middle of the road but yellow lines and dead armadillos." His message – stay away from the political middle unless you want to get run over. For better or for worse, I have accepted the challenge of cheating fate in the middle of the road. Perhaps, after reading these essays, you may want to join me on that lonely patch of asphalt.

A note on the organization of this book. It's pretty simple – I have arranged these essays, which were published in *The Huffington Post* from 2008 to the end of 2013, in reverse chronological order. They follow the course of events from Obama's first election through his second, and comment on the various national debates that consumed the country during that time. I hope they will provide a valuable perspective on interesting times. As the famous Chinese curse says, "May you live in interesting times." These essays chronicle what has been a very interesting time.

Hoyt Hilsman

Pasadena, California

The Republicans and the Radical Minority

December 2013

As 2014 begins, the Republican party faces another year of intraparty warfare, with Tea Partiers and other conservatives, along with their wealthy backers, vowing to continue their war on moderate and establishment Republicans, who are promising to fight back aggressively. As both parties should have learned by now, these kind of intraparty fights, initiated by a radical minority, generally have more losers than winners, with the nation itself often in the loser column.

Recent examples include the Goldwater debacle in 1964 for the Republicans and the McGovern trouncing in 1972 for the Democrats. While there is an argument that these disasters -- the result of intraparty warfare -- ultimately strengthened the political parties, it can also be argued that these elections represented serious setbacks for the nation by weakening the opposition party and loosening the restraints on the majority party. And there is one overwhelmingly tragic example of intraparty warfare that was devastating for the nation and which led directly to the bloodiest conflict in American history -- the Civil War.

As the country approached the presidential election of 1860, the nation was deeply divided, but so was the Democratic party, which consisted of factions from the slaveholding South and more moderate Democrats from the Midwest and Northeast. In April, 1860, the Democrats gathered for their convention in Charleston, South Carolina, a hotbed of pro-slavery sentiment. Senator Stephen Douglas of Illinois, a moderate Democrat who supported the Missouri Compromise, which permitted territories to choose whether they would be slave or free, was the leading contender for the nomination.

However, a sizeable pro-slavery faction rejected Douglas, proclaiming that he was not sufficiently pro-slavery. Led by Alabama Congressman William Yancey, who denounced Douglas as a "traitor," the pro-slavers drafted a party platform that endorsed the Dred Scott decision and called for legislation to protect slavery. When the moderate Democrats rejected the platform, the pro-slavery delegates walked out. This effectively shut down the convention, which later re-convened in Baltimore and nominated Douglas.

While this might have been viewed as a defeat for the pro-slavery faction, it was in fact the goal that they hoped for. Their plan was to splinter the Democratic party -- whose nominee was highly favored to win the White House -- and thus provoke the secession of the Southern states. The favored Republican nominee was New York Governor William Seward, who held strong anti-slavery views. If the

Democratic party split and Seward was elected, it would boost the pro-slavery faction's hopes for secession.

As they went to their convention in May of 1860, the Republicans understood the scheme of the pro-slavery Democrats, and ended up passing over Seward and nominating the more moderate Abraham Lincoln in hopes of averting a full-scale confrontation. However, Yancey and his cohorts were in no mood to compromise, and managed to convince most Southerners that any Republican, even the moderate Lincoln, was out to destroy their way of life.

In fact, Yancey and his supporters had argued that Southern secession would be a peaceful transition. In his fine chronicle of the period, *Year of the Meteors*, author Douglas R. Egerton describes the optimism of the Southern secessionists, very few of whom expected war. He quotes one Southern firebrand as saying "You may slap a Yankee in the face and he'll go off and sue you, but he won't fight." They were, of course, very wrong.

While we are unlikely to face another civil war in the current climate of cultural and political warfare, it is worth bearing in mind that extreme minority factions can do serious damage to the nation as a whole when they pursue a strategy of burning down the political house in hopes of building a new one.

In another fine historical book, *The Great Debate*, Yuval Levin outlines the intellectual debate between Edmund Burke, who advocated a practical, middle road for social change, and Thomas Paine, who believed in more radical action for change. For Republicans especially, since they consider themselves the intellectual heirs to the Burke tradition, it is worth paying attention to the risks of succumbing to the schemes of a radical minority.

The Deeper Issues in the Shutdown Crisis

October 2013

As the partisan warfare in Washington continues over the government shutdown and looming debt ceiling, it is important to examine some of the deeper issues in this ongoing battle. Whether it is the fight over Obamacare or the deficit or government spending priorities, there is a consistent theme to all of these fights. Ever since the beginning of the Great Recession in 2007, the drumbeat from both Democrats and Republicans has been to "restore jobs to the middle class," or some variation of that theme. Despite their different perspectives and approaches, both political parties express the same goal over and over, which is to protect the standard of living of middle class Americans. The only problem is that this goal is both unrealistic and misleading.

In his recent book *When the Money Runs Out*, economist Stephen D. King argues that after an extraordinary growth spurt in the 1950's and '60's, and a series of boom and bust cycles at the end of the twentieth century, Western economies, including the United States, have entered a period of extended decline. In the first decade of the twenty-first century, growth in Western economies averaged just 0.9 percent, less than half the rate of the previous two decades and less than a third of the growth rate of the "golden age" of the '50's and '60's. King offers a number of reasons for the decline, some of which have to do with errors by Western governments, but most of which seem to have been beyond the control of political leaders.

So what is the lesson for America? If it is true that we have entered a period of general economic decline, is "protecting the middle class" a realistic goal? Wouldn't it be more sensible to address our current situation rather than be looking in the rearview mirror, pining for the good old days? It is true that optimism is a key component of the American character, but so is common sense. Furthermore, optimism is based on a hopeful but realistic vision of a future that may be different - although not always better - than the past.

The mistake that our political leaders from both parties are making is in promising more than anyone could possibly deliver, and then blaming the other side for our problems. It is misleading for politicians to promise a return to the unusual economic conditions of the past, when they know full well that this is not possible. Of course, politicians tell voters what they want to hear, but at some point, we need a frank national conversation about the situation that we face.

The truth is that both parties are offering sensible solutions to the decline that we are confronted with. The Republicans are correct that we need to squarely address our national debt and government spending. The dollar cannot reign supreme forever, and eventually our creditor nations will put the squeeze on us to clean up our balance sheet. At the same time, the Democrats are correct that we need to strengthen the social safety net for all of our citizens as we face the prospect of economic decline. A nation that does not forcefully address income inequality, injustice and a host of other civic issues does not have much of a future.

The irony in this era of partisan warfare is that on the policy front, the differences between the Democrats and the Republicans are not that great. Democrats generally acknowledge that we need to get our balance sheet under control, while the most Republicans want to preserve important social programs like Medicare and Social Security. In truth, a combination of these policies are exactly what the country needs to confront the economic decline that we are experiencing.

The further irony is that both Democratic and Republican politicians keep repeating the false mantra of protecting the middle class. In fact, the middle class has suffered and will continue to suffer in the future, due largely to economic factors that are beyond the control of our government. It makes no sense for Democrats and Republicans to blame each other for the plight of the middle class, when there is little anyone can do about the general economic decline. Except, of course, to acknowledge that this is the reality of our situation and set about to actively work together to make the best of it.

Japan entered a period of economic stagnation in the 1980's which it has never fully recovered from. While many faulted government policies, King points out in his book that much of the stagnation was a result of factors beyond Japan's control. Through a combination of individual self-sacrifice, social cohesion and a sense that "we're all in this together," the Japanese people have weathered the storm. In fact, when I asked a Japanese friend to compare today's Japan with the go-go period before the 1980's, he replied "Things are better now." What he meant was that despite economic hardships, the nation was more coherent, more caring and perhaps even happier than during economic boom times. While there are vast differences between the American and Japanese experiences, one can hope that in a few years or decades, despite economic hardship, we can also say "Things are better now."

The Government Shutdown and Death of the Old Order

October 2013

The shutdown of the federal government led by the right wing of the Republican Party confirms what some observers have seen as the transformation of American politics, which began in earnest with the Great Recession and the election (and re-election) of Barack Obama. While many have decried this era of partisan gridlock and warfare in Washington, others see it as the most hopeful sign in decades that the conservative ideology which took hold in the Reagan era is finally doomed to extinction.

Although most Americans are exasperated by the stalemate in Washington and by the extreme tactics of the Tea Party, students of history will recognize the symptoms of generational change. With older, conservative white male voters losing their dominant electoral position to younger, minority and female voters, the Tea Party movement represents an extreme reaction to the demise of the old political order. As has happened over and over again throughout history, the old order will fight to the death to preserve their power, even as it slips away.

In their insightful book *Millennial Majority*, authors Morley Winograd and Michael Hais point out that the 2012 election was a watershed of political change and that the emerging electorate is more socially tolerate, more favorable to government and more supportive of international multilaterialism than the older, more traditional American voters. They also point out that any transformation of a political order involves real struggle as the dying order fights for survival.

Seen in the light of history, the calls for President Obama and the Democrats to be more conciliatory towards the Republicans are misguided. After the wake-up call of the 2012 election, the Republicans are clearly in survival mode. The shutdown of the government is only one example -- restriction of voting rights in North Carolina and Texas and opposition to a path to citizenship for illegal immigrants are further examples of their desperate fight. As is clear from these recent battles, there is no reason to negotiate with people who are threatening to bring down the government.

It is more apparent than ever that history is on the side of the new politics of social inclusion, economic progress and international multilaterialism. The narrow interests of a dwindling group of ultra-conservatives will not slow the march of history. This will be a prolonged and costly struggle, but the end result is clear. Ironically, by engaging President Obama in these high-stakes battles, the Republicans may be cementing his legacy as a truly transformative president.

Good Cop, Bad Cop and the Syria Crisis

September 2013

Since the Syria crisis began, there has been lots of talk from both sides of the political spectrum about how America should not be the "world's policeman." That naturally raises the issue who will be the world's policeman in the future, or whether the world even needs a cop on the beat.

Beginning with Woodrow Wilson's League of Nations and later the United Nations, the idea was that an international organization would take on the role of global policeman. The vision was that somehow an international body might supersede more narrow nationalistic interests and act for the common good of humanity. That hasn't worked out very well, and the UN has been dismissed and derided by most of the global community, including many in the United States.

Perhaps one of the other major powers wants to volunteer for the part. Vladimir Putin's recent op-ed piece in The New York Times suggests that Russia may be vying for that role, or at least to be a more active part of the police force. While China hasn't yet stepped forward to take on the assignment, they may soon have to become a cop, if only to protect their global economic interests. And there may be other nations waiting in the wings.

So who will be the world's policeman? And does the world really need a cop on the beat? Many would argue that we don't need a global cop, that regional conflicts are inevitable and the best policy is to stand back and let the regional players settle disputes on their own. Of course, that does set the stage for all kinds of horrible human rights abuses, including genocide, use of terrible weapons and other horrors.

There is at least a valid argument that these things will happen anyway, and there is very little a world policeman can do about it. The problem with that argument, however, is that regional conflicts very rarely are self-contained, especially in the globalized world we now inhabit. In the case of Syria, for example, the civil war clearly impacts the entire region, and threatens to have even broader consequences for the world as a whole.

Another alternative is to have the major powers - ostensibly the United States, China, Russia and the European Union - share the role of world cop. But how well would that work out? We see from the Syrian crisis that the major powers regard the crisis more as an opportunity to jockey for power and influence than a chance to solve a humanitarian tragedy. And the national interests and public sentiment of each of the major powers -including the United States - holds more sway than broader humanitarian concerns.

Up until the end of the Cold War, America didn't have to fret that much about playing the role of world's policeman. It simply did whatever it could to block the influence of the Soviet Union, and to a lesser degree, China. But after the breakup of the Soviet Union and the boom in Chinese economy, America's strategy got muddled. The terrorist attacks of September 11th and the wars in Iraq and Afghanistan were the culmination of that muddled strategy.

So where does that leave the United States today? Do we give up our role as the beat cop? After all, it has been a tough, expensive job with very few good outcomes. What's more, the world pretty much resents us for playing that role. So why not quit trying to save the world on focus on our own problems at home, of which there are many?

There are a couple of good reasons not to beat a hasty retreat. First, as bad as America has been in its role as world cop, there are some much worse alternatives. There is no way that having Russia or China play a leading role as global policeman would be any better. Take a look at the human rights records of both these major powers, and you can well imagine what a world policed by them would look like.

Second, and equally important, is the fact that the well-being of our own country depends on America taking a leading role in the world. In a highly competitive global economy, the United States can no longer depend on its position as an economic powerhouse to maintain our way of life. Russia, with its vast energy resources, and China, with its booming economy and huge labor pool, are serious rivals to America's economic power, not to mention the emerging nations like Brazil and India.

General Carter Ham, retired head of the US Africa Command, recently remarked on the "strong connection" between military security and strong economic policy. Ham's comments were aimed at getting our economic house in order, but the inverse is also true. A strong American economy - and by extension a vital global economy - depends on a stable and safe world where markets can operate freely and peacefully. America, with its history of openness and respect for individual freedom and opportunity, must continue to play a major role in protecting those values of freedom and openness. Whether or not we decide to be the world's cop, we still want to be part of the police force.

On the Brink of War

August 2013

The United States is once again on the brink of war in the heart of the Middle East. It seems certain that we will launch an attack on the Syrian regime in the near future, most likely in the form of air strikes on Assad's air force, munitions depots, communications command and other military infrastructure. It is also possible that the U.S. will impose a no-fly zone, although that would be difficult to enforce.

The model for this action seems to be Libya, where a stalemate was developing between Col. Gaddafi's forces and the rebels before the intervention of the United States and its allies. Although it took longer than many observers foresaw, the result was ultimately positive to the extent that it tipped the balance in favor of the rebels, who were primarily homegrown nationalists.

The Syrian civil war is much more complicated, since it not only is unclear whether a victory by the rebels would be positive for the U.S. and its allies in the region, but it also involves a large number of actors who have much greater stakes in the outcome than they did in Libya. The Saudis and the other Gulf States are engaged in a regional conflict with Iran, as is Israel, albeit for different reasons. Turkey, Jordan and Lebanon are being destabilized by a flood of refugees. And the Russians and Chinese have their own interests in the conflict, especially as it relates to their competition with America.

While the necessity of some kind of military intervention -- if only symbolic in nature -- is now evident, the risks are enormous. The chances for American intervention to spark a wider regional conflict will certainly increase. Much depends on the reaction of Iran, which could range from an attack on Israel to an increase in support for terrorist plots. The Saudis and the Gulf States seem to believe that a showdown with Iran -- whether diplomatic or military -- is inevitable, and they are pouring resources into the area to counter Iranian influence.

Meanwhile, the American public -- weary of war and struggling with a weak economic recovery -- are opposed to military intervention. Prior to the recent chemical weapons attack, a Reuters/Ipsos poll showed that 60 percent of Americans opposed intervention, while only 9 percent would support it. Even when asked if they would support an attack after chemical weapons were used, the respondents opposed intervention by a margin of two to one. It is clear that the Obama administration will have to work hard to gain support for even a limited military intervention.

As we enter into yet another war in the Middle East -- one that could provoke an even larger regional conflict -- it is important for Americans to be clear-eyed in their expectations for our role in the conflict. We should expect the unrest in the Middle East to be a complex and lengthy, perhaps lasting for generations. Too many nations, along with religious, ethnic and political groups, have competing interests in the region for it to be settled by any single military or diplomatic action.

It is also important -- as it was in Iraq, Afghanistan and Libya -- to remain focused on the long-term principles and interests of the United States and the international community, and not get caught up in the emotions of the moment. The failures in Iraq and Afghanistan -- and in the struggle against terrorism since 9/11 -- were in large part due to an impulsive desire for revenge and retribution rather than a cool-eyed, objective decision about what was in the best interests both of America and the world.

As we plunge into yet another war in the Middle East, there will certainly be events in the coming weeks and months that will send our blood boiling, horrify our consciences and spur us to find quick and simple solutions. But there will be no simple solutions. We will have to deal with the pain and uncertainty of the region and the suffering that will inevitably occur. There is much we can do to relieve that suffering, but, in the end, we cannot prevent it.

For the past five years, our nation has been distracted by those on the far right -- from the Tea Party activists to Republican politicians who have cowered in the face of primary challenges from their right. Their stonewalling on issues from Obamacare to gun control and immigration, along with the refusal to engage in reasonable compromise on even the most modest proposals has deepened and widened the partisan divide in our country.

Even though most Americans are moderate in their views, the extremes of the political spectrum get the most attention and, therefore, more clout. And let's be honest about this -- the far right has much more influence than the far left. The Tea Partiers and their ilk hold far greater sway over the Republican party than the far left does over the Democratic party. Even the Democrats derided as "socialists" by the right pursue much more moderate and flexible positions than the ideological right.

Moving Past the Far Right

June 2013

As a country, we have wasted too much time over the past five years fretting over the concerns of a small group of right-wingers. From health care to immigration to gun control, America should have long ago tackled these problems with common-sense, practical approaches, rather than getting mired down in ideological debates. Everyone from the business community to our international allies recognizes that this ideological bickering and the resulting national stalemate only harms America.

So what can we do about it? First and foremost, ignore the ideological drumbeat from the right. We've heard them out, considered their views and even incorporated some of those views into our national consensus. But we must also realize that ideologues will never be satisfied or tamed, and we should quit trying.

But what about the Republican party, which seems to be held captive to the far right? That is a more complex issue, since we need a responsible opposition party to craft a reasonable consensus. For the moment, that responsible opposition does not exist. Congress is deadlocked, and the hands of the president are largely tied in addressing national issues. To make matters worse, the midterm elections of 2014 don't promise any grand reshuffling, with the Republicans expected to maintain their majority in the House.

So are we destined, for at least several more years, to national policy deadlock? Probably, yes. However, there are some silver linings to this cloud. And they lie in the states. In my state of California, for example, we now have a Democratic governor and legislature that are moderate in their approach to social issues and responsible on fiscal matters. California is passing stricter gun control laws, promoting education reform, pro-actively implementing Obamacare, and taking measures not only to improve the lives of its citizens, but also to compete effectively in a global marketplace. In other words, California -- and states like it -- are moving ahead, despite the national policy gridlock.

Compare this with many of the "red" states, who are spending their time and resources fighting Obamacare, gun control, immigration reform, gay marriage and other issues that are near and dear to the hearts of the far right. Who would have imagined that state governors would be turning down money from the federal government to improve the health and welfare of their citizens? It demonstrates the triumph of ideology over common sense.

For a long time, those of us in the "blue" states have fretted over how to free our red-state brethren from the clutches of the far right. I know, those in the red states will argue that they are not in the clutches of anybody, but they are wrong. By far the majority of Republican elected officials in red states were put there by the fewer than 10 percent of the citizens who voted in the Republican primary. And those 10 percent are overwhelmingly to the far right of the spectrum.

We can no longer expend time and resources trying to bridge the red state/blue state gap. On a national level, it will happen naturally as the older, white Republican voters are outvoted by a younger, minority and more progressive electorate. But in the meantime, we as a nation should not be held captive by a red-state contingent who are themselves held captive by a tiny minority of their own voters.

One can expect the policies of the red-state politicians to backfire in the near future. Their stubborn positions on Obamacare are self-defeating, and eventually they will have to be bailed out by the federal government -- which means the rest of us in primarily blue states. We should be willing to help our fellow citizens if that is the price of preserving our nation. Certainly none of our disagreements are worth fighting another Civil War over. However, in a time when our greatest challenge is to pull together to compete in a global economy, we should not waste another minute trying to mollify the concerns of a reactionary, ideological few.

The Political Suicide of Kelly Ayotte

May 2013

Senator Kelly Ayotte this week became the poster child for callousness in her confrontation with Erica Lafferty, the daughter of the slain principal of Sandy Hook. In a single stroke, Ayotte committed perhaps the swiftest and most devastating act of political suicide in recent history. Sure, she is likely to serve out her term which ends in 2016. The chances of a successful recall are slim, and she can expect lots of support from the NRA and the gun industry. But, as a practical matter, her political career is over.

Her Senate colleagues are likely to have very little do with her -- keep your eyes peeled for a photo of a fellow Senator giving her a big hug or headlining a fund-raiser. Ayotte is headed for the political outback -- on the bullet train. It's not simply that she voted against background checks for gun purchases -- which the overwhelming majority of her constituents support. It's that she had the temerity to lecture Ms. Lafferty, in mostly patronizing tones, all on national television.

Even if Senator Ayotte cast her vote in good faith, I am pretty sure she didn't want to become the poster child for the NRA and the gun industry. In one fell swoop, she has singled herself out as a major spokesperson on a highly emotional issue on which the vast majority of her constituents -- along with a sizeable majority of Americans -- disagree with her. Even worse, she has firmly ensconced herself inside the fringe of the Republican right, who are holding virtual parades in her honor at this very moment. This is decidedly not where a New Hampshire politician wants to be.

I am very curious -- along with lots of others in the political world -- about who gave her the political advice that led to this vote. Certainly, it may have been a matter of deep conviction (I am giving Ayotte the benefit of the doubt here), but surely some political calculus came into play. Who in their right mind would advise a politician to vote against the majority of her constituents on an emotional issue like the mass slaying of children? Ayotte can blabber all she wants about mental health concerns (since when have Republicans become concerned about mental health issues?), but this isn't really about mental health or background checks, for that matter.

This vote was about children gunned down at an elementary school and, by extension, about the larger issue of gun violence in our country. Senators who voted for background checks were signaling to the public that gun violence was a serious enough issue to regulate gun purchases in some small measure. Senators who voted against the bill were signaling that gun rights trumped any concerns about gun violence. By the way, this was exactly the way Erica Lafferty phrased her question to Ayotte when she asked whether the burden of her mother's murder wasn't greater than the burden of background checks for gun purchasers.

I suppose that Ayotte's political advisors may have made the argument that she needed to curry favor with her base -- the fifteen percent of Republican voters who vote in primaries and tend to be more hard right. But that would be a foolish argument, since her task as an elected Senator is to court more moderate voters -- in other words, the bulk of her constituents. Perhaps Ayotte was afraid of the NRA. That would also be a mistake, since it is unlikely that the NRA or the gun industry can rescue her from the onslaught she now faces.

Not only is Ayotte's political future in the toilet, but her ongoing effectiveness in the Senate is likely to be nil. She will certainly be shunned by all but the most Red-State senators, and her media image is permanently trashed. There is very little positive good that she can do for her constituents in New Hampshire as she fights off the deluge of criticism from around the country and inside her state. Late-night comedians and pundits will feast on her decaying political carcass. Perhaps it might be time to consider resignation? Give it a couple of months, then withdraw gracefully.

Getting Real About Gun Violence

May 2013

The debate in America has shifted from gun control versus gun rights to the larger issue of preventing gun violence. Whether gun control advocates like it or not, the Constitution guarantees citizens the right to bear arms, with certain restrictions. And whether gun rights advocates like it or not, society is moving in the direction of more restrictions on sales of guns and the types of weapons that can be sold and possessed.

But as a number of commentators have pointed out, the pro-gun vs. anti-gun debate does not address the realities of gun violence in America and the most critical issues in preventing it. For example, David M. Kennedy, director of the Center for Crime Prevention and Control at the John Jay College of Justice, points out in an op-ed in the Los Angeles Times that the vast majority of gun crimes and violence involve everyday handguns, which would not be affected by any of the current gun control proposals

Furthermore, Kennedy argues that gun violence is concentrated in mostly poor and minority neighborhoods, and is driven by a tiny number of people -- about 5 percent of the young men in the most dangerous neighborhoods. Citing initiatives like Operation Ceasefire in Boston, Kennedy believes it is possible to identify these "hot" groups and individuals, and then intervene with a variety of law enforcement and social service measures. The Boston effort cut youth homicide by two-thirds and all homicide by one-half.

Another important factor in gun violence is understanding the risks of gun ownership, particularly of handguns. Virtually all significant studies conclude that having a gun in the home -- especially a handgun -- greatly increases the risk of accidental or intentional death or injury to family members or other innocents. While some gun owners argue that they need guns for self-defense, the statistics show that for every self-defense homicide in American homes, there are 1.3 accidental deaths, 4.6 criminal homicides and 37 suicides. In other words, a gun in the home is much more likely to accidentally kill, to murder or to be used in a suicide than in self-defense.

The NRA and other gun rights groups argue that they are strong advocates of gun training and safety. If that is true, then they should partner with other groups -- private and governmental -- to promote the safe use of guns, as well to educate the public on the risks of gun ownership. There is no way that we as a society can legislate sensible behavior around gun ownership, which is protected by our Constitution. People must take individual responsibility in the ownership and use of firearms. However, as an effort to prevent the tragedy of gun violence, there should be much greater resources devoted to educating Americans about the risks of gun ownership and the realities of gun violence.

The Republicans' Obama Problem

May 2013

By attacking the president on every front -- from Obamacare to Benghazi -- the Republicans are following a tried-and-true formula for a party out of power, especially during a second-term presidency. They did it with Clinton, and the Democrats did it with Bush. But this is a different era -- and a very different Republican party. Their brass knuckle assaults on Obama are sure to backfire and damage the Republicans more than Obama and the Democrats.

Here's why. The Republican party is now engaged in a civil war among a number of factions -- social conservatives, fiscal conservatives, evangelicals and the Tea Party. They disagree on a host of issues from gun control and immigration to deficits and military spending. But what they all seem to agree on is their dislike -- even hatred -- for Barack Obama. However, in their blind fixation on attacking the president, what the Republicans don't seem to understand is that Obama will never again be up for election.

Sure, it's good political sport to go after your enemies. But you have to be careful when you choose those enemies. It is true that Democrats were often vicious in their criticism of George W. Bush. But it is also true that the Bush presidency -- with the fiasco in Iraq and the onslaught of the Great Recession -- was viewed as a disaster by most Americans. It seriously tarnished not just Bush, but the Republican party brand. President Obama, on the other hand, despite the controversies over Obamacare, has not only led the country out of Iraq (and soon Afghanistan), but also out of the Great Recession. However doggedly the Republicans go after Obama, they won't be able take away from those accomplishments in the minds of the majority of Americans.

Barring some major catastrophe, it is unlikely that the Democratic brand will be damaged very much by the record of the Obama administration or by the attacks from Republicans. It is true that the Republicans will likely keep the House in 2014, largely because of stubborn incumbency rates and chronic gerrymandering of districts. They may have a shot at retaking the Senate because of the vagrancies of the election cycle, but even that is looking somewhat less likely.

So who will the Republican attacks on Obama damage most? The answer, as surprising as it may seem, is the Republicans themselves. By attacking Obama, the Republicans are throwing red meat to their base, which is an increasingly small and extreme group of right-wingers. The danger of tossing red meat to a tiger is that it becomes even more aggressive. Translation: The Republican base --

especially the Tea Partiers -- may decide that even the hint of compromise with Obama is treason, and to be punished by a political death sentence.

We saw this happen in the last election cycle, when right-wing Republicans offered up extremist and often dangerously incompetent candidates, who won their primaries (thanks to low turnout from more moderate voters) and then lost to Democrats in the general election. Whenever a party decides to circle the wagons and fire within, it is a political bloodbath, as the Democratic party witnessed in the Vietnam and post-Vietnam era.

The leaders of the Republican party are under constant pressure to exploit every scandal or trumpet every failure, great or small, of the Obama administration. By doing so, they are playing a very dangerous game that could further split their party and do permanent damage. With Rand Paul already making noises about a run for the presidency -- and some Tea Partiers raising the specter of an independent candidacy -- Republican leaders ought to be very concerned about adding fuel to those fires. Not to mention the fact that all the self-righteous outrage from the Republicans does not go over well with most Americans, who want to see action, not attacks.

For the sake of the country, I would hope that the partisan attacks on the president are toned down to a reasonable level. But as a supporter of the president and, more importantly, the progressive policies of the Democratic party, I have to admit to a certain amount of pleasure at the misguided attack tactics of the Republicans, since they only help the Democratic cause in the long run.

How Roger Ailes and Fox News Screwed the GOP

March 2013

In 1996, when Rupert Murdoch hired Roger Ailes, a Republican political consultant, to launch Fox News, his mission was simple: to provide a counterpoint to the "left-wing bias" of the national media. But Murdoch and Ailes weren't simply on a right-wing propaganda crusade; they also aimed to capitalize on what they viewed as a largely underserved sector of America: the "silent majority" that had been dismissed by the cultural elites who ran the media business.

Though this "silent majority" seemed reasonably happy with the mainstream media, Murdoch and Ailes seized on the rising popularity of right-wing talk radio and imported its message -- and strident tone -- into cable television. They not only made sure that Americans got the right-wing message; they paid up to $11 per cable subscriber to make sure that Fox News had a prominent place in the cable universe. The result was not only a financial bonanza for Fox but a generation of right-wing propaganda in the guise of journalism.

The fact is that Fox caught the news-as-entertainment wave and shrewdly played on the entertainment value of political conflict to garner huge ratings. However, the main casualty in the rise of Fox was truth, as more and more Americans viewed politics through Fox's bare-knuckled, conspiracy-theorizing, partisan perspective. And despite the network's "fair and balanced" claim, Fox increasingly converted viewers to their one-sided ideological take on the world.

Although Fox News has become the chief messenger and opinionator for the Republican Party, it may ultimately bear much of the responsibility for tarnishing the GOP brand with most American voters. When political parties embrace demagoguery and half-truth (and let's be honest, that's what Fox is doing), they do so at their own peril. Once you've sacrificed truth in the name of ideology, you've opened Pandora's box. The GOP opened that box, and what flew out was the tea party.

Although one might argue that the tea party was at least in part a grassroots expression of cultural discontent, it is hard to deny that the flames of that discontent were fanned not only by right-wing talk radio but by the constant ideological drumbeat of Fox. With only the thinnest journalistic veneer, Fox championed an extremely partisan ideology that blossomed into -- what else? -- political extremism.

The irony is that the biggest long-term beneficiary of the Fox propaganda machine has been the Democratic Party and, most especially, President Obama. After almost 20 years of Fox's pseudojournalism, the country has shifted distinctly to the center-left, and Republicans are viewed as a party of reactionary, old, white guys, hostile to everyone from Latinos to women. Fox worked hard to gin up their viewers -- conservatives, Reagan Democrats, Southerners and rural Americans -- and it worked, sometimes too well. A sizable group of those voters have now moved further to the right and into the ranks of the tea party.

Having lost the popular vote in the last several presidential elections, the GOP is trying valiantly to rebrand itself with the American public. But it faces a civil war within its ranks from tea partiers, libertarians and other conservatives who seem to care less about winning elections than about ideological purity. As the GOP leadership knows, that is a recipe for disaster. This is not quite what Murdoch and Ailes had in mind when they launched Fox News. They may have made a bundle of money in the meantime, which may have been their primary goal all along, but the end result has been a disaster for the Republican Party and the conservative movement.

Gun Violence and America's Image in the World

January 2013

As someone who has traveled extensively in Asia, Latin America, the Middle East and Europe over the past several years, I have experienced a nearly universal opinion of America society as violent and crime-ridden. Most Americans would probably be surprised by this view, but it is no wonder, with the drumbeat of stories about horrible massacres, rampant crime and widespread gun violence. Admittedly, much of the world's perspective on our society is gleaned from sensationalist media and popular films, television and video games, but nevertheless the vision of America as a chaotic and violent place is firmly etched in the minds of much of humanity.

While there may have been a time when we could shrug off the opinion of the rest of the world, we can no longer afford that luxury. When we were the pre-eminent global economic force, we didn't have to worry about what foreigners thought of us, as long as they bought our products, which they did in abundance. And in a time when over half the nations of the world were under the yoke of totalitarian systems, America's spirit of freedom and economic vibrancy was a beacon for people everywhere, even if they worried about our penchant toward violence.

However, as Tom Friedman and others have pointed out, the world is flattening. While America is still the leading economic power, it is now competing with the BRIC countries (Brazil, Russia, India and China), as well as the Eurozone and many other rapidly developing nations in Asia and Latin America. Although the United States still has significant advantages in terms of productivity, creativity and skills, we can no longer assume that those advantages will put us in the strongest competitive international position.

One of the greatest dangers to our future prosperity is that the rest of the world will see us as a society in decline. In the jungle of the global economy, no one is in greater danger than the wounded lion -- everyone is out to get him. But it is not our material wealth -- or our military might -- that are coming into question. It is our health as a society. Who wants to visit or invest in or even do business with a country that is violent and chaotic, where the government is in gridlock and the public divided? One need only cite the example of Mexico, which has suffered a huge blow to tourism and a substantial decline in economic growth because of drug violence and government inaction.

For most of our history, America has had the reputation among foreigners as the Wild West, but decades of assassinations, drug violence and horrendous gun massacres (not to mention three unsuccessful wars), have pushed the United States into the category of a failing society in the eyes of much of the world community. This not only adds an air of uncertainty to our position in the global marketplace, it also provides propaganda fodder for our enemies.

So what role does gun violence play in the diminished image of the United States, which was once viewed as the shining city on the hill by much of the world? The high-profile massacres, not to mention the epidemic of gun violence in our inner cities, are a potent symbol of where America has gone wrong. What is worse, the American government and public, in the eyes of the world community, appear to be largely indifferent to this humanitarian crisis.

Piers Morgan of CNN has been criticized by gun rights advocates when he expressed utter bewilderment at America's antiquated and ineffective gun laws. Nevertheless, his bewilderment is shared by most of the citizens of the civilized world. How, they wonder, can America sit idly by while its citizens are gunned down in the streets, and even more recently, in its schools? We have to concede that they have a point.

Certainly, preventing gun violence is more complicated than gun control. The roots of the violence are clearly deeper -- in poverty, social conditions, mental health failures, popular culture and a host of other areas. However, the tools of gun violence are not complicated -- they are guns. It is beyond comprehension that civilians in a modern, civilized society must be as heavily armed as we are, often with weapons that are capable of mass killing. And it is even more unbelievable that our government has, until now, done little to address this terrible crisis.

In many ways, the Newtown school shootings represent a crossroads for America, not simply in terms of gun violence, but also in terms of our future as a nation. Because the world is rapidly changing -- from the streets of Beijing to the barrios of Sao Paulo -- we must be part of that change. The world is flat and we must become increasingly part of that world if we are to thrive and prosper. Addressing the critical issue of gun violence can serve as a potent symbol of our willingness to address the challenge of change. We can no longer afford to abstain from the standards of the rest of civilized world, nor is there any moral justification for doing so.

Republicans Should Listen to Gingrich

January 2013

House Republicans should listen to Newt Gingrich, who is warning that holding the country hostage with debt ceiling brinksmanship will backfire. Gingrich, who after all was responsible for twice shutting down the government, argues that the American people won't stand for Congress jeopardizing our national credit by refusing to pay for bills that have already come due. The former Speaker wisely believes that the Republicans should more carefully pick their battles, and this isn't one they are likely to win.

Gingrich suggests that the Republicans take the smarter course, which is to propose their own spending cuts in the form of a continuing resolution; in effect, put their cards on the table. He asserts that since 75 percent of Americans favor spending cuts to reduce the deficit, the Republicans will have a much better argument if they fight for those cuts rather than threatening to ruin the nation's credit and provoke a deeper recession, possibly on a global scale.

Of course, Gingrich is only half right about public support for cuts. While a large majority favor reducing spending cuts in the abstract, when it comes to specific cuts to Medicare, Social Security and other entitlement programs, public support drops considerably. Still, Gingrich is right that the morally responsible approach for the Republicans would be to put forth and fight for the proposals they believe in, specifically entitlement cuts, rather than arguing for less spending while refusing to put forward specifics. And, above all, Gingrich correctly makes the point that it would be politically foolish and dishonest to hold the debt ceiling as a hostage.

One other interesting point that Gingrich made recently: Republicans need to get over Obama. The president won reelection and will be in the White House for four more years. He is not running again and there is no reason for Republicans to go after him personally -- although that still seems to be high on their agenda. If they were smart about it, they would realize that all second-term presidents have at most two years to exercise their political power. After two years, every second-term president effectively becomes a lame duck, and there is no reason to believe Obama will be any different.

However, the Republicans seem to be hell-bent on continuing their anti-Obama crusade, even though it harms their party and their cause much more than it hurts Obama or the Democrats. So while Newt Gingrich represents much that has been wrong with the Republican party for the last 20 years -- and is as responsible as anyone for the extreme partisanship in Washington today -- he has clearly learned some lessons from the past, lessons that the current crop of House Republicans would be well advised to pay attention to.

Time for an American Spring?

January 2013

Okay, it's clear they don't get it. After several elections, the Great Recession and lots of moaning and groaning about the stalemate in Washington, our national leadership still can't manage much progress on the issues that are most important to our future as a country. As one commentator recently pointed out -- it's not the fiscal cliff that is our greatest threat, but the breakdown of public trust in our government.

What can be done? The political system -- a quagmire of political gerrymandering, special interest lobbying and a torrent of campaign spending -- has officially hit a wall. The short-term solutions that have been gussied up to kick the can down the road are largely irrelevant. We've passed the point of urging the political class to stop bickering and come up with some real answers. They are clearly aren't going to get there on their own.

It's not as if there hasn't been a hue and cry from many quarters. The Occupy movement on the left and the Tea Party on the right have been challenging our political leaders to be more responsive to the citizenry -- even though they represent the extremes of the political spectrum. Inside-the-beltway pressure hasn't worked either. The Simpson-Bowles commission, which at least tackled the tough problems, was quickly thrown under the bus by both sides of the aisle. And no amount of hectoring from the media, the business community or non-partisan activist groups worked either.

Is it time for an American Spring? Few people would suggest an effort to overthrow the government or a wave of mass demonstrations. But the business-as-usual tools of democracy don't seem to be working. Citizens have a chance to vote every couple of years, but recent elections have done nothing to shake up the leadership. Ninety-five percent of members of Congress are routinely reelected if they manage to stay out of jail or avoid a sex scandal. The primary system is essentially rigged so that a handful of the most zealous, uncompromising voters get to choose the elected officials. And billions of dollars flow into the coffers of candidates who can be most helpful to the wealthy elite, corporations or special interests. At the same time, the media thrives on the 21st century version of yellow journalism, focusing on the sensational and irrelevant.

So how about a nationwide citizens' strike to get the attention of the political class? It wouldn't have to be a massive, European-style demonstration. It could be something as simple as a one-hour (or 15-minute) citizen protest where people shut off their computers, close their office doors, stay away from the malls and avoid other routine, non-essential tasks. If just a few million Americans joined in such a protest, it would certainly get a lot of attention and might even shake the politicians from their stupor.

What would be the goal of a citizen strike? Simple. Send a message to politicians that we are fed up with kicking the can down the road. Let's at least have an honest conversation about the issues that face our country at this critical time -- unemployment, global competition, tax and spending reform, education, the environment and the deficit. It's not about left or right, it's about the future of our country. No need to get swept into dead end wedge issues -- let's look at what really matters to most Americans -- their jobs, their health, their kids' education and their future.

When could a citizen strike happen? The sooner the better. How about Tuesday, Jan. 15 at 2 p.m. EST?

Mitt Romney, Big Bird and American Creativity

October 2012

Mitt Romney's comment in the first debate about defunding Big Bird was the fodder for lots of jokes, but it has more serious implications, not just for public funding for the arts, but for the future of America's global competitiveness. As America's economy has become less focused on man1ufacturing and more on innovation, design and global branding, much of America's future will depend on a vital, innovative cultural and artistic environment in our country.

What Governor Romney -- and apparently many of his conservative supporters -- do not understand is how everything from iPhones to automobiles depend on design and branding, which are crafted by people trained largely in the arts. What sells iPhones is both their form and function, which were brilliantly designed by teams of creative people. In virtually every field, from Hollywood to the high tech, America's primary global advantage is its creative work force.

Millions of Americans now work in creative fields, from graphic design and advertising to entertainment and technology. It is estimated that one in three new jobs in the United States will be in creative fields in the future. But these creative workers don't simply appear magically from the soil of America. Nor are they nurtured by the laissez-faire policies of conservatives, who seem to believe that any spending to support the arts or arts education is money wasted.

There are two critical factors to maintaining America's global advantage in creativity. The first, of course, is support for creativity in the form of arts education and arts institutions in general. This is not simply about money, but about an emphasis on creativity in our schools and other institutions. While many countries have workforces who excel in precise engineering or flawless production, the United States is the global champion in creative endeavors. This has not happened by accident, but is a result of our emphasis on individual initiative and imaginative thinking, which have been prized not only in our schools but in our society as a whole.

The second critical factor is related, but less specific. Our culture has long been forward-thinking, restless and often chaotic. Out of this creative chaos have come many of the greatest innovations in technology, science, entertainment, the arts and economics. While there is very little that can quiet this creative American spirit, the kind of cultural conservatism that Romney espouses does pose a real threat to American innovation and creative competitiveness. The idea that we should stifle not only Big Bird, but also the other fertile laboratories for creativity -- especially those in the classrooms -- is ultimately self-destructive.

During the Reagan administration, there was an active effort to quash counterculture and other innovative movements -- not by heavy-handed repression, but by swamping our country with a regressive, cheery group-think about American exceptionalism. There is nothing wrong with American optimism -- it's a bedrock value -- but the Reagan administration seemed antagonistic to any creative expression that strayed from that lockstep optimism.

We are in an even more precarious situation today than we were in the Reagan era when it comes to creativity in our society. American conservatives now seem to equate creativity and artistic expression as a political threat. Any art form beyond quilting, country music and landscape painting is not only frivolous (and possibly blasphemous), but also a political or even existential threat to conservative values.

Clearly, the danger is not that a Romney administration would shut down artistic expression. However, the emphasis on traditional values at the expense of creativity poses a serious threat to not only American society, but to our economic competitiveness. If we stifle creativity by strangling arts and education budget, and stunt innovation with an emphasis on politically correct conservative values, we risk losing the tremendous advantage we have in the global marketplace.

My Family's Missile Crisis

October 2012

Fifty years ago this week, I was a high school freshman in Washington, D.C., playing on the basketball team, rehearsing for the school play and dreaming about having my first girlfriend. That same week, my father was working especially late at the office, and being very tight-lipped about what was going on at work during October 1962.

Two years earlier, my dad, Roger Hilsman, had been appointed by President Kennedy to be Director of Intelligence and Research at the State Department. Most of his work consisted in supervising research analysts in drafting policy papers -- pretty boring stuff in the eyes of his 14-year-old son. However, I was impressed when, shortly after his appointment, several men in white coveralls installed a secure White House phone in my parent's bedroom. We children were warned, in the sternest of tones, never to touch that phone.

On the evening of October 15, 1962, my dad got a call on the secure phone from the Deputy Director of the CIA. The subject was the U-2 photos of nuclear missiles in western Cuba. Over the next week, the Cuban Missile Crisis not only plunged the world into turmoil, it also had a profound impact on me and my family. While my dad always worked long hours, during that week he seemed never to be home.

As the week progressed, rumors began to appear in the press about a crisis brewing. In one of the few conversations I had with my dad that week, I remember asking him while he was shaving what was going on. Of course, he wouldn't answer as I rattled off a series of possible hot spots -- Berlin? India? Israel? Only when I suggested Cuba did he pause for a moment, though certainly not long enough to let the secret slip out.

For the rest of that long and anxious week, as the extent of the missile crisis became public, I was swept up with a mixture of fear and pride -- fear that nuclear war was imminent and pride that my father was somehow part of this unfolding drama. There was near panic among my classmates as they feared that that their young lives -- and perhaps the whole world -- could come to an abrupt and violent end. I vividly remember our history teacher leading us in a prayer for peace on the eve of President Kennedy's speech announcing the quarantine of Soviet vessels. And I sat riveted to the television watching UN Ambassador Adlai Stevenson confronting the Soviet ambassador. What I did not know at the time was that my father was sitting nearby, having delivered the U-2 photos to Stevenson.

For me, my family and the rest of America, much changed over that week in October. As a nation and a world, we had stared down the barrel of nuclear destruction. It was real and tangible. Schoolchildren were led into bomb shelters with the expectation that nuclear war was imminent. Everyone in America -- even young people -- understood that the human race had come closer to annihilation than ever before in history.

The aftermath of the Cuban Missile Crisis was one of relief, but also of the loss of innocence. We could no longer trumpet war as a solution to political conflicts or as a vehicle of simple revenge. In a nuclear war, there would be no victors, only victims. We realized how vulnerable we were to the decisions of not only our own leaders, but the leaders of our adversaries. And we understood how fragile and precious was peace.

In the 50 years since that week in October, there has been some progress towards peaceful solutions to human conflict, despite the tragic wars in Vietnam, Iraq and Afghanistan, not to mention the scores of other bloody civil conflicts around the world. Since the Cuban Missile Crisis, human beings everywhere have understood that another global conflict would likely lead to destruction on a scale that humankind has never before witnessed.

There has been modest progress in the control of nuclear weapons and other weapons of mass destruction. Most nuclear states have signed international treaties, and there have been efforts to slow nuclear proliferation. Still, there are many nations who either possess or are actively developing nuclear and other weapons of mass destruction. There is no doubt that countries like Iran must be prevented from developing nuclear weapons, and nuclear nations like Pakistan must do more to make sure those weapons are secure.

However, it seems clear that 50 years after the Cuban Missile Crisis, we are not much closer to banishing the threat of nuclear war. This means that our highest priority must not simply be on preventing the use of nuclear weapons, but rather on the active, vigilant and ruthless pursuit of peace. Peace will not simply settle gently and magically over our planet. It will only come through the grinding, frustrating and persistent pursuit of peace as the ultimate goal.

For each of us that means holding our leaders -- and the leaders of the rest of the world -- accountable for the pursuit of peace. It means making peace a priority in our everyday lives and in the faith and values that each of us holds dear. It does not mean weakness in the face of aggression or threats. But it does mean looking always to the better angels in our nature to find solutions to the challenges of human conflict. Fifty years after that terrifying week in October, 1962, we must never lose sight of those angels.

It's the (Electoral College) Math, Stupid!

October 2012

Despite the considerable doom and gloom from Democratic quarters and the tightening poll numbers in the wake of the first presidential debate, it is important to remember that President Obama has a distinct advantage where it counts most -- in the Electoral College. While it may seem wonky to dig into electoral votes when it's more fun to listen to the pundits opine on the daily tracking polls, the electoral votes are what really count. To paraphrase Bill Clinton, it's the math, stupid. (Thanks to Real Clear Politics interactive Electoral College map, it's a pretty easy to do the math).

As we all know, the large majority of electoral votes (398 in 39 states) are already in the safe column for one or the other of the candidates. In the remaining eleven states, there are roughly 140 up for grabs. However, many of those states have fewer electors, which leaves the big three battleground states as the most important prizes. Those are, of course, Florida, Ohio and Virginia.

By most calculations, if Obama wins any one of these three states -- each of which he won by between three and six points in 2008, he will likely to be re-elected. Either Florida or Ohio would put him over the top in terms of pure numbers, and a victory in Virginia would indicate that independents are voting for him and he would likely pick up a win in one or more of the smaller battleground states - thus giving him a victory.

But what if Obama lost all three major battleground states -- Virginia, Florida and Ohio? Would that mean certain defeat? Not necessarily. Wins in New Hampshire, Iowa, Colorado and Nevada -- all of which gave Obama margins of nine percentage points or more in 2008 -- would still clinch a victory. The post-debate polls in Colorado and Nevada have Obama and Romney virtually tied, while Obama is ahead by three points in Iowa and four points in New Hampshire.

States like Florida, Ohio, New Hampshire and Iowa have traditionally been evenly divided between the parties, while changing demographics in Virginia, Colorado and Nevada have meant wide departures from historic patterns that favored Republicans. What this all comes down to is not the outcome of the debates or expensive ad campaigns. What matters above all is the turnout in the battleground states. If the Obama campaign can deliver the ground game and turn in victories in at least one of the three major states -- or wins in the smaller swing states -- then the numbers will add up to a victory. Despite all the talk-show pontificating, it's still all about the math.

We Democrats Shouldn't Get Overconfident

September 2012

As any football coach will tell you, the greatest danger a team faces is overconfidence - especially when they have a lead in the fourth quarter. The recent surge by President Obama in the polls, particularly in the battleground states, is certainly good news, but it also runs the risk that his supporters will become overconfident. Mitt Romney had a terrible month in September, which revealed many of his weaknesses as a candidate, not to mention the fissures within the Republican party. However, we should remember that re-election campaigns are a referendum on the incumbent and Obama's approval ratings have been below fifty percent for most of the campaign - a real danger zone for incumbents.

There will be another important factor in the final weeks of the campaign - the role of the media. While the Republicans have been accusing the media of a bias against Romney, the media tone may actually tilt against Obama as election day approaches. As Neal Gabler pointed out in a recent op-ed in *The Los Angeles Times*, the media treats elections like sporting events - they want a close contest. So the narrative may shift in October to make the race seem closer, which may in turn affect the momentum of the campaign, the polls and even the outcome.

With expectations for Romney at a low point, any sign of life from the Romney campaign may be trumpeted by the media as a "comeback." So if Romney scores a couple of points in the debate, the media will tout the revival of his campaign and talk about how the "momentum is shifting." On the other hand, any slight misstep by Obama (and they are bound to be some) will be blown up into a campaign stumble. Since Romney is now trailing, we should also expect his campaign to become more aggressive and vigorous. There will likely be a new "look" to the campaign which the media will seize on as part of the "comeback" narrative.

While all this media buzz may be viewed as so much irrelevant chatter, it could have serious consequences for the election. If the "shifting momentum" narrative gets a lot of play, that could encourage Republican turnout. At the same time, overconfidence by Democrats could depress turnout (even more than the Tea Party's effort to keep Democratic voters from the polls). And the "shifting momentum" story could influence independent voters to go with Romney.

The bottom line is that the election is still close. Even though President Obama does have a chance to break out with a strong victory, the likelihood is that the election will be close and will be decided by voter turnout, particularly in the battleground counties of the battleground states. If those of us who support Obama decide that the election is in the bag, become overconfident and fail to deliver every possible Obama voter, then victory may still be in doubt.

The Disappearing Second Term?

June 2012

The recent disastrous jobs report, coupled with the ongoing crisis in Europe and the precipitous stock market decline, are terrible omens for President Obama's reelection. Again and again, incumbent presidents have been defeated by economic forces over which they have virtually no control. The global financial meltdown and the euro crisis were entirely out of Obama's hands, but if history is any indicator, he will become a victim of the economic crises. It is possible that an economic miracle will suddenly reverse all the political damage, but with only five months to go before the presidential election, that window is closing rapidly.

There will certainly be lots of Monday-morning quarterbacking among Democrats if Obama is defeated. One could argue that health care reform was a laudable fight that was launched at the wrong time, and that the White House wasted political capital on that effort. A stronger argument, however, might be Obama's failure to confront the broader dimensions of the financial crisis. Perhaps if he had taken the FDR approach -- fighting hard from day one for economic recovery as his sole mission -- he might have been given more slack by the electorate. It is worth remembering that FDR was re-elected in the depths of the Depression after little or no economic progress, largely because he was seen as a tireless, bare-knuckle advocate for the average person. Had Obama cultivated that image, he might be better equipped to fend off the challenge of the super-wealthy Mitt Romney.

While it is clearly too early to write off an Obama second term, it might be time for Democrats to begin developing a strategy if Obama appears headed for defeat. Unfortunately, most scenarios look pretty grim for the Democrats. Although there are a number of Tea Party Republicans in the House who are vulnerable, a Romney victory would probably mean that the House would remain in Republican hands. And the Democrats will have to fight hard to retain the Senate. In the next few months, Democrats will have to decide whether to retool their efforts away from keeping the White House and more into holding onto seats in the Senate, and perhaps picking up a few seats in the House. Not a pretty picture.

The larger question is what a Romney presidency might look like and what role the Democrats can play when the Republicans control the White House, along with one or possibly both houses of Congress, a situation that is very rare. All this comes at a time when more Americans than ever identify with the more progressive social and political ideology of the Democratic party as opposed to the far-right Tea Party-leaning Republicans. However, when the economy falters -- or even worse, when deep structural fissures appear -- voters invariably hold the White House incumbent responsible, and his party suffers the consequences.

Price Fixing is Bad for Both Readers and Authors

April 2012

I'm not crying crocodile tears over the decision by the Justice Department to sue Apple and the major publishing houses for price-fixing, especially since it will benefit not only readers, but also authors. But I am bewildered by the hue and cry from the publishing community by the argument that setting artificially high prices on e-books is somehow good for everybody.

The truth is that this dispute is not about saving literature or the sanctity of the literary world, it is about the publishers' business model. Since the advent of digital technology, the book business -- along with the music business, the film business and a slew of other traditional businesses -- has been broken. When the major publishers had a chokehold on both book production and distribution, they could reap huge profits, which were generally not shared with authors, and certainly not passed along to consumers.

Let's take the example of authors' royalties. Authors are generally paid around 10% of the price of a hardcover book and 6-8% for paperback book. For a hardcover book originally priced at $30 (minus up to 30-50% discount for many books), the author generally gets between $2-3 per book. For paperbacks, it's under a buck.

Now compare that with what an author can make if he or she publishes the book independently and offers it on Amazon as either a print-on-demand hardcover, paperback or e-book. Depending on how many copies are printed, the cost of producing a hardcover book is between $5 and $10 (the print-on-demand cost for a single 300-page hardcover). For a $30 book, that means a profit of between $15 and $25 per book, depending on discounting.

E-books can be even more profitable for authors. At virtually no cost, authors can upload a book to Amazon and offer it for sale. If the sale price is $9.99 (the price the publishers call untenable), then the author can earn over $7 per e-book (three times the publishers royalty for a hardcover). Even at $4.99 per copy, the author is making more than publishers would pay.

So what is it exactly that publishers are offering to authors that they would accept a pittance in royalties compared to what they could make on their own? The publishers argue that they offer editorial, production, marketing and distribution services that no small publisher or independent author can provide. But that is patently false. To begin with, for an investment of under $2000, an author can hire highly professional freelance editors and designers to design the book.

What about production costs and expertise? With today's technology, authors can work with very competent print-on-demand companies and produce a hardbound book for around $10 (which still leaves them with a profit of $15 per book, compared with royalties of two bucks.) If the author decides to print 5000 copies, the cost drops considerably. And, by the way, an author can get the book produced in a month or two, compared to the two years it often takes major publishers.

Then how about marketing? The truth is that, with exception of celebrity authors, the major publishing houses do virtually no marketing on behalf of authors. The first question every author is asked is "What is your platform?" Which means "How many followers do you have you will buy this book?" If your platform is not big enough to cover the publishers' costs, you probably won't get published.

Then what about distribution to bookstores? In that area, publishers have an advantage, but it is disappearing. More and more, distribution companies are looking at the potential market for handling distribution with independent authors and small publishers. But, more importantly, the brick-and-mortars bookstore market is a dwindling.

Which brings us to e-books. E-books are the fastest growing segment of the publishing business -- arguably the only growing segment. Readers of e-books read more books than those who read only printed books. And while some traditionalists have argued that e-books will spell the death of printed books, the truth is that most e-book readers generally read both print and e-books.

In the face of these new realities, it is hard to make the argument (as the publishers and some authors are doing) that having lower prices for e-books is a bad thing, either for readers or for authors. The publishers have argued in the past that that high prices for books subsidize publication of authors who would not otherwise get published. That suggests that the publishers are in a charity business, which they are decidedly not. And it is hardly true anymore, when the bookshelves are crammed with celebrity biographies, vampire romances and flimsy self-help tomes. The reality is that authors who would not otherwise get published can now get published in a variety of forms -- e-book, print-on-demand and other forms -- and make three to four times the money per book.

Despite all the fuss about diversity, literature and the "unique" aspects of book publishing, it is a business like any other, and must operate within the realities of the marketplace and the law of the land. Artificially raising prices simply to preserve an outdated business model is not the way to preserve the critical importance of books and reading in our culture. Perhaps the major publishing houses will suffer - they may even wither and die (although I doubt it). But books will go on in many new and old forms. And readers - and authors - will be all the better for it.

This article originally appeared in *The Chicago Tribune*.

America's Missed Opportunities in Latin America

April 2012

President Obama's visit to the Summit of the Americas in Colombia underlines America's failures to confront global and economic challenges as we focus inwardly on our own political squabbles and endure partisan gridlock. It also demonstrates our blindness toward developments around the world -- particularly in our own hemisphere -- as we squander important opportunities to engage with some of the most dynamic economies and societies.

Most Americans still regard Latin America through the myopic lens of the past -- repressive dictatorships, left-wing ideologues and drug cartels. In reality, Latin America is a diverse, rich and rapidly growing collection of nations and peoples. Once burdened with uncontrollable debt, most of Latin America has emerged from insolvency to impressive economic growth.

Brazil, the leading economic dynamo of Latin America, is now the sixth largest economy in the world and number two in the hemisphere behind the United States. It has taken its place along with China, India and other rapidly growing economies in aggressively diversifying its economy, with global investments across the spectrum of industries and continents. No longer simply a major Latin American power, Brazil is a global economic and political force.

Other Latin American countries, notably Colombia, Chile, Argentina and Peru, are shedding their difficult and often dark pasts to emerge as regional economic powerhouses. A growing middle class throughout Latin America has made it a vital market for a host of goods and services. Brazil, for example, has a GDP of over $2 trillion, with imports of $182 billion annually. Despite difficult visa requirements and long waits, 1.2 million Brazilians visit the U.S. each year, spending on average $5,000 per visit.

The center-left governments of Latin America, which replaced the right-wing (or left-wing) dictatorships of the past, have steered a steady course of economic responsibility and political moderation. These governments have been generally popular and have been able to achieve political and economic reforms that had been impossible in the past. This, in turn, has led to strong economic growth and wider participation in increasingly global markets.

China, Russia and other global economic powers have been aggressively participating in Latin American growth -- investing in everything from factories and coal mines to banks and insurance companies. Meanwhile, the United States remains largely sidelined in the economic and diplomatic arena, even though it maintains strong security relations with Latin American governments. Trade agreements -- like the one recently signed with Colombia -- have been painfully slow to be completed.

One problem -- in addition to the political stalemate in this country -- is most Americans' outdated view of Latin America. Mexico, the one Latin American country which has bucked the trend, slipping into violence, political dissension and economic difficulty, seems to have an undue influence on Americans' perception of the Southern hemisphere countries. In fact, Latin America has much more in common with quickly developing countries in Asia than it does with Mexico.

Certainly, Latin America is plagued with many critical problems including economic inequality, drug trafficking and deficits in education and infrastructure, but it has clearly emerged from a dark and sometimes dismal economic and political past. Latin America presents enormous opportunities for the United States in terms of economic and political cooperation, but we continue to squander these opportunities as we squabble among ourselves over issues like immigration, drug policies and, most importantly, our role in the global economy. As in other areas of the world, it is time for the United States to wake up to reality and take constructive, cooperative action to promote our economic, political and security interests in Latin America.

The Republican Path to National Failure

April 2012

A very clear argument is emerging in this year's presidential campaign: higher taxes for the wealthy and investing in the middle class versus lower taxes for the rich and cutting middle class entitlements. The Republicans argue that lowering taxes and cutting entitlements will stimulate growth -- a dubious proposition at best. The Democrats argue for more fairness in the tax code and long-term investment in the middle class.

While the logic of this debate, especially in a democracy, would seem to fall to the greatest good for the greatest number, the Republicans insist that economic growth depends on lower taxes and cutting spending. Although they may have a point that we must reduce spending in the long run, drastic cuts are never helpful for economic growth in the short term. And their argument that high taxes on the rich inhibit growth is clearly contradicted by history -- strong growth in the '50s and '60s was coupled with tax rates for the rich at 75 percent and above.

But there is a more serious question than taxes or economic growth at work here. It is the issue of political leadership and the future of our democratic society. In the recent book *Why Nations Fail: The Origins of Power, Prosperity and Poverty*, authors Daron Acemoglu and James Robinson argue that nations fail because of the unrestrained greed and ignorance of the political classes. Societies that are more inclusive and have restraints on the wealthiest and most powerful also do better economically.

The authors cite the differences between the absolutism of the Spanish monarchs in the 17th and 18th centuries versus the relative restraint on the British crown after 1688. The powerful Spanish elites became dissolute and corrupt, ultimately destroying their empire, while the British system flourished, mostly because of the rise of a merchant class. Rejecting the "exceptionalist" arguments of the Tea Partiers or "geographic good fortune" arguments made by Jared Diamond and others, Acemoglu and Robinson cite the corruption of a powerful, unrestrained ruling class as key to the failure of nations.

Americans have always been reluctant to see their society as rooted in a class system, or primarily ruled by tiny elites. But the financial crisis has laid bare many of the realities of our economic and political system, and it is not a pretty picture. Economic inequality has become more pronounced and, more ominously, political power is now concentrated in a wealthy elite, a trend that was cruelly accelerated by the Supreme Court's ruling in *Citizens United*, which opened the floodgates of political power for the rich.

The most pressing thesis of *Why Nations Fail* is that economic success depends on a political system -- and in particular political leadership -- that is the most inclusive. This is especially true in the emerging global economy, where technology has opened global markets, allowing greater access to millions of people. Greater inclusion has meant more growth, and nations around the world are benefitting.

However, in the United States, we are still having a debate not about greater inclusion, but about increasing the power and exclusivity of the economic and political elite. From immigration to health care and education reform, the Republicans are arguing for restricting access not only to the poor, but chiefly to the middle class. At the same time, they are arguing for a greater concentration of wealth among the elites through everything from lower tax rates and unrestricted campaign donations to limiting access to health care and educational opportunity.

The misguided Republican political and economic philosophy lies in a twisted and unrealistic view of America's history and political system. America has always succeeded when it took an inclusive approach to its political and economic system. From restraints on monopolistic trusts to welcoming immigration policies to social welfare programs such as Social Security and Medicare, America has focused throughout its history on the broadest possible political and economic participation. With the new economic and political realities of the global economy, it is more important than ever that we reject the Republicans' stunted and myopic view of our country.

Conservatives, Health Care and Fire Departments

April 2012

President Obama recently characterized the Republican governing philosophy as nothing but "social Darwinism." "If you get sick, you're on your own," Obama said. "If you can't afford college, you're on your own. If you don't like that some corporation is polluting your air or the air that your child breathes, then you're on your own. That's not the America I believe in. It's not the America you believe in."

While this speech may be viewed as a bit of campaign hyperbole, it does lay out the essential philosophical differences between the political parties. A purely objective look at the American political system, of course, would reveal that it is pretty much in line with other liberal democracies, albeit with a rightward cultural slant. So true social Darwinism is not in the cards; however, global economic realities are forcing us as a nation to decide how we will govern ourselves going forward.

The current fight is over health care reform. The insurance-based individual mandate, originally a conservative idea, has raised the philosophical issue once again. While the wrangling over the "mandate" language has dragged in distracting constitutional issues, the federal government clearly has the power to tax citizens to pay for services like health care, even though conservatives would prefer the market-based, insurance model, which has so far failed miserably.

This philosophical argument over the role of government has been going on in America since colonial days, and in Europe long before that. One of the most interesting debates was over firefighting services. In ancient Rome, there were public fire services, paid for by taxpayers, but later societies in Europe left people to fend for themselves. However, as European cities grew in the Middle Ages and whole municipalities were destroyed by fire, people wanted help in putting out the fires.

Both volunteer and private fire brigades sprang up in the 18th century; however, by the 19th century, insurance companies saw a market for private fire insurance, and that market boomed. But the problem remained that if you didn't get fire insurance, no one came if your house caught on fire. While most people didn't care if someone else lost their home to fire, they became concerned that if no one arrived to put out the fire at their neighbor's house, then their own house would catch fire and burn. Thus the first public fire departments were born in the United States around the time of the Civil War.

Still, conservatives were not convinced, and there have been efforts to privatize fire services ever since. Some are based on insurance -- the insurance giant AIG, for example, now provides private fire services to policy holders. Other efforts involved privatizing fire departments, which have been successful in some cases, and failures in other cases. In the end, it all comes down to what kind of fire services people want, and what they are willing to pay for.

The same goes for health care. What do we want, and what are we willing to pay for? Do we want only those who are insured to get medical care? If so, what do we do about the social and economic costs of 50 million uninsured Americans? If not, how much are we willing to pay to treat those who cannot afford to pay? These are century-old arguments that came up in debates over income taxation, Social Security, Medicare and virtually every other program that either levies taxes or bestows benefits.

Again and again, it comes down to what we want, and how much are we willing to pay for. Unfortunately, the debate over health care -- and over other government programs through the years -- has not focused on that simple question. Conservatives don't seem to be willing to pay for anything, while liberals don't want to cut anything. So we get a stalemate. Politicians bicker and slam each other, all the while kicking the can down the road.

Eventually, as with fire services, people realize that if their neighbor's house burns down, then their house could catch fire, and they finally decide to do something to solve the problem. Sure, the solution is never perfect, but whatever they decide will be better than watching both houses burn. Only the most self-destructive society wants that. And, hopefully, America has not -- and will not -- descend to those self-destructive depths.

Supreme Court Ruling Against Affordable Care -- A Blessing in Disguise?

March 2012

While the Supreme Court wrestles with how to untangle the constitutional complexities of the Affordable Care Act, the politics are becoming crystal clear -- and they may ultimately benefit those of us who would like to see affordable, high-quality health care for all Americans.

As we have learned from the arguments in the case, the central issue is the individual mandate, which the opponents argue exceeds Congress's power under the Commerce Clause. While most of the Court's cases since the early 19th century would support the constitutionality of the act, the conservative shift in the Court suggests that the mandate could be struck down.

The question then becomes whether the mandate is severable from the rest of the law. Common sense says that it is not, since there would be no way to pay for health care reforms without everyone participating in the health insurance pool. It would seem unlikely that the Court would strike down the entire ACA, but even if it finds that the mandate is severable, it would likely doom the law in its present form.

If the Court did make the mandate severable, then the new Congress would probably take up the issue after the election in an effort to save the law minus the mandate. If the Republicans maintain control of the House, then that would be an effort in futility, since they have vowed to repeal the law in its entirety and would have no reason to try to salvage it.

This is where the politics gets interesting. If the Court's decision makes the law unworkable, then Americans will be faced with a stark choice. If they vote in the Republicans, then health care reform is doomed -- specifically all the provisions that have already gone into effect, including mandatory coverage for existing conditions and insurance for children up to 26 under their parents' policy. If they vote for Democrats and the House goes back to Democratic control, then health care reform has a decent chance of passing.

The question then becomes what kind of health care reform do we want? With a Democratic House, there are a lot more choices. So why go back to a clunky and flawed act that may have constitutional infirmities? Why not institute some form of universal health care that even the opponents admit does not have the constitutional problems that exist under the current act? The Republicans have already conceded that they will do nothing to promote health care reform, so why not call their bluff and go after real health care reform in the shape of universal coverage?

Presented with a choice of universal health care coverage -- essentially extending programs like Medicare that already work and are popular -- and doing nothing, American voters seem likely to support a program that tested and proven, rather than wander back into the wilderness of half-measures and partisan bickering. A Supreme Court decision against the mandate -- if not the entirety of the ACA -- may prove to be a blessing in disguise in achieving comprehensive medical care for all Americans.

Don't Underestimate Santorum

February 2012

While the rise of Rick Santorum in the national polls of Republican voters may cheer many Democrats, who believe that he would be a weak general election candidate, there are some signs that Santorum may be a more formidable opponent than most people think. There are a couple of reasons for this, based on different election-year scenarios.

If the economy improves, with the unemployment heading downward for several months this spring and growth picking up, then Obama has a significant advantage going into November. As an incumbent president, Obama has a built-in advantage, not to mention the resources that incumbency can bring. And, simply put, if things are getting better with the economy, then voters are less likely to switch horses in midstream. The only caveat would be a pickup in inflation, particularly a spike in gas prices.

However, if the economy stays flat, or there is even a small downturn, then Obama will be in for a real fight. Romney, as a former businessman running on his experience as a CEO, may be able to score some points over Obama, but Romney has not yet generated a lot of enthusiasm in the Republican base, which is vitally important in close elections.

Which brings us to Santorum, who has generally been dismissed as an extreme social conservative who has great appeal to the hard right of the Republican party, but not much chance in a general election. However, Democrats need to rethink the general view of Santorum, not based so much on his extremism or lack of popular appeal, but rather on the complexion of the electorate and the mathematics of the Electoral College in a close election.

Looking at the Electoral College map, there are several factors that favor Santorum, even if he were to lose in the popular vote. Obama got 370 electoral votes in 2008, which would seem like a comfortable margin when 271 votes are required to win. However, many of those votes came from states that traditionally vote Republican, like Virginia and North Carolina, or from swing states that went Republican in the 2000 and 2004 elections, including Florida, Ohio, Missouri, Iowa, Indiana, Minnesota, Colorado, New Mexico and Nevada. All together, those states will account for 134 electoral votes in 2012, more than enough to put a Republican over the top.

In very close elections, there are two key elements to victory. First, a fired-up base which Obama had in 2008 and Santorum would likely have if he gets the nomination in 2012. But even more importantly, it is a few independent voters in a very few swing counties in a few swing states that usually determine the outcome of the presidential contest. And those are the voters who will consume virtually the entire focus of a close campaign, particularly in the last six weeks as the candidates race from county to county in Ohio or Missouri or Florida, chasing down the few undecided voters in key districts. So who are those few independent voters in the swing counties of the swing states?

It is impossible to tell with great precision, since many voters register as independents but vote predictably with one party or the other. About two-thirds fall into this category -- splitting evenly between voting Democrat or Republican. That leaves only one-third that are truly independent voters, open to voting for either party depending on the candidate. This group also tends to be moderate to conservative in their ideology. While they may hold moderate views on social issues, they tend to be pro-business and anti-big government.

So where would Santorum stand with these voters, who will determine the outcome of a close presidential election? While much depends on how Santorum stands up to the negative attacks within the Republican party, Santorum has some reason to be optimistic about his chances with this handful of voters who may choose our next president. While Democrats will decry Santorum's views on social issues, and the Republican base will rally behind him, most truly independent voters may largely ignore his extreme conservatism on social issues, simply because they don't really care about the wedge issues.

If that is true, then the independent voters may lean towards Santorum because of his economic conservatism -- even if it is little more than empty rhetoric. Again, this will depend largely on the state of the economy, since these independent voters are more likely to view Obama favorably if the economy is showing signs of recovery -- and are less likely to want to dump a White House incumbent. However, it is a danger sign for Obama that, according to a Pew study, 47 percent of independents who voted for Obama voted for George Bush in 2004, and 25 percent of them voted for a Republican candidate in the 2010 Congressional elections.

While it may sound crazy to many Democrats who view Santorum as an extremist of the worst stripe, he probably will not be regarded by independents in the same way. Unlike Rick Perry, Michele Bachmann, Herman Cain and Newt Gingrich, all of whom proved to be irresponsible and impulsive in their public demeanor as well as their political ideology, Rick Santorum has so far run a disciplined and smart campaign that shows him to be an experienced political operator. Even his outrageous statements about everything from gay marriage to contraception and the role of women in combat seem based on careful political calculation rather than simple impulse.

Although some may argue that by raising the flag of wedge issues Santorum will alienate general election voters, that argument may be too simplistic. Santorum certainly understands that in a close election, both Democrats and Republicans will return to their traditional voting patterns. That means that Virginia, North Carolina, Indiana and Missouri, along with possibly Colorado and Nevada -- all of which went for Obama in 2008 -- will likely go Republican. That leaves the big prizes of Florida and Ohio -- not to mention Santorum's home state of Pennsylvania -- to clinch the election.

If Democrats fall into the trap of engaging Santorum on the social wedge issues or simply branding him as an extremist, they may be ceding a big advantage to the Republicans in the fight for those few crucial independent voters in the swing states. Those independent voters are unlikely to base their votes on social issues, no matter how extreme a candidate's views. For those voters, the key is the candidate's positions on big government and the economy -- and perhaps most importantly the demeanor and perceived character of the candidate. Obama -- who certainly can compete well against any of the Republican candidates -- will need to confront Santorum vigorously on all those fronts.

Death Penalty for Bankers?

February 2012

Would you support the death penalty for bankers or corporate executives who cheat clients, customers or the government out of millions, or even billions, of dollars? That's the question that is raging through China these days as 30 year old multi-millionaire Wu Ying, once one of the richest women in the country, was sentenced to death for swindling $57 million from investors.

While $57 million sounds like chump change compared with the $65 billion that Bernie Madoff stole from investors, the Chinese take both economic crimes and the death penalty quite seriously. Around 4,000 people are executed each year in China, some for economic crimes, and the death penalty has the general support of the public.

The problem, of course, is the issue of selective enforcement. The crimes that Wu Ying is accused of committing -- including "underground banking" (lending money outside the officially sanctioned government system) -- are widely practiced in China and are only selectively punished. And the death penalty seems to be employed arbitrarily against a variety of citizens, including in some cases political dissidents.

Fewer than half the countries in the world -- and a minority of nations -- continue to apply capital punishment. The European Union bans capital punishment and the United Nations has passed resolutions calling for a global ban on the practice. Yet the United States and China -- arguably the most powerful nations in the world -- continue to employ capital punishment, although in markedly different ways.

The United States spends billions of dollars to enforce the death penalty. The state of Maryland, for example, estimated the cost of pursuing a total of five executions to be $186 million. California spends $114 million per year prosecuting and housing death row inmates, and estimates that the cost of thirteen executions over thirty years has been $250 million per execution. China, on the other hand, which dispenses with much of the niceties of due process, can say that it has a much more streamlined and cost-effective system.

What about the effectiveness of the death penalty as a deterrent? People have argued for years that the death penalty can be an effective deterrent against crime, but the facts certainly don't do much to support that argument. Extensive research into the "deterrence effect" show that it has very little weight. Studies show that most murders, for example, are committed in the heat of passion or under the influence of drugs or alcohol. The likelihood of execution is one of the last things that murderers consider when they kill someone.

The fact that China employs the deterrence argument in the case of economic crimes raises an interesting question for Americans, who have generally accepted the policy of giving white-collar criminals who steal billions nothing more than a slap on the wrist. Even though a few of the most egregious offenders have ended up behind bars, an argument could be made that if they had committed the same crime in China, the Bernie Madoffs of the world would be facing a firing squad. And perhaps a few Wall Street bankers would be asking for a last meal.

The truth is that the deterrence argument probably doesn't work much better for economic crimes than it does for murder or other capital offenses. While the Chinese government hopes to send a strong message to the business community to play by the rules, the fact is that Wu Ying was clearly singled out because she crossed some powerful people in the Chinese power structure. Although her conviction -- and possible execution -- will send a chill through the hearts of Chinese entrepreneurs, it will likely do little to stem the practice of underground banking and loan sharking, not to mention the greed and corruption of elements of Chinese society.

There may be a lesson for Americans here. The outcry over the minimal -- or non-existent -- punishment of American bankers and Wall Streeters is clearly justified. The idea that the rape and pillage of the American financial system, not to mention the American public, by a bunch of overpaid bankers and corporate executives, who after getting a bailout from American taxpayers rewarded their misdeeds with millions in bonuses, is galling to say the least. And it is tempting to contemplate sentencing these criminals to life in a prison cell, or even an ignominious death.

However, as in China, the solution to the problem is not simply to lock up or execute the offenders, although justice would certainly dictate much harsher punishment than was meted out to those bankers whose greed and deceit cost us so many billions and nearly wrecked our financial system. No, the answer is to reform the system so that criminals can no longer benefit from their misdeeds. And only the federal government has the power to carry out those reforms.

The Republicans have argued that government regulation of the financial industry will stifle the free market, but nothing could not be further from the truth. The reforms during the administrations of both Theodore Roosevelt (a Republican) and FDR (a Democrat), which regulated financial activity in new and unprecedented ways, was greeted with dire warnings from the financiers and robber barons about the collapse of the American economy. However, the reforms actually led to unprecedented growth in financial markets and the American economy.

The Obama administration has taken a few tentative steps in the direction of greater regulation of financial markets and institutions, but much more needs to be done. However, as long as politicians depend on the good graces of wealthy people and institutions to stay in office, real reforms will never take place, and those who game the system, or even violate the law, will swindle the rest of us with impunity. We may long to put the bums in jail and throw away the key, but until the government becomes an honest, impartial referee in the financial markets, there will be more swindlers taking the place of those we locked up.

Bringing Up Bébé, *Idonomics* and the American Dream
February 2012

Journalist Pamela Druckerman's new book *Bringing Up Bébé*, which generally praises French child-rearing techniques, is causing quite a stir. Druckerman, who lives in Paris, writes that French children sleep through the night at three months, eat well-rounded meals at regular hours (no snacking) and are generally much better behaved than their American counterparts. And French moms apparently have a much easier, calmer sense of authority and aren't as harried as American moms.

Druckerman, who used to write for *The Wall Street Journal*, has provided yet another tome in the growing library of "foreign-moms-are-better" literature. How can we forget Yale Law School professor Amy Chua's *Battle Hymn of the Tiger Mother*, which extolled the virtues of her Chinese mom tough-love philosophy? All of this seemed to be designed to make American parents feel downright pitiful.

While Americans debate the value of discipline and self-control -- clearly throwbacks to the Puritan philosophy -- the French prefer to talk about "education" of children, which is more in line with their Enlightenment principles. One of the keys to childhood education is learning to delay gratification, which is accomplished not by harsh measures, but by the firm, calm exercise of authority. French children are not permitted to interrupt adults in the middle of a conversation, and are not allowed to eat except at prescribed mealtimes. And French parents are shocked that American children can go to the refrigerator any time they please for a snack.

Although childrearing approaches can be endlessly debated -- and seem to be in constant flux not only from culture to culture, but also from generation to generation -- the impact of childrearing on society is clearly enormous. Starting in the 1950's with Dr. Benjamin Spock's parenting books and later in the 1960's and '70's with the generation of baby boomers coming of age amidst rapid social change, Americans became increasingly permissive -- and at the same time overly attentive -- to their children.

There has been much handwringing over helicopter parenting, hyper-parenting and all the rest. Whether it is the result of our overindulgent parenting styles, or our conflicts about discipline and boundaries, it is absolutely clear that American society has lost much of its traditional sense of self-control. We see it in everything from the mountainous level of personal and national debt to the high rates of divorce and addiction, and from the excesses of the media to our rancorous political partisanship.

In my recent book, _Idonomics: How the Pleasure Principle is Destroying the American Dream_, I cite the landmark study by Walter Mischel, an Austrian-born research psychologist who conducted an interesting experiment at Stanford University involving four year-olds and marshmallows. He offered the children a tempting choice -- they could have one marshmallow right away, or if they waited a few minutes, they could have two marshmallows. Videos of the kids struggling with deferred gratification show their anxiety as they cover their eyes and fidget anxiously, trying to avoid eating the delicious treat that is right in front of them. Most of the kids couldn't hold out more than three minutes before eating the marshmallow. About thirty percent, however, were able to delay gratification for about fifteen minutes.

Mischel's experiments, along with his follow-up of his subjects over the next thirty years, spawned a whole range of studies into the mechanics and sources of delayed gratification. Mischel's findings that the thirty percent of children who were able to resist temptation had higher academic achievement and better personal relationships later in life also generated great controversy. This in turn led to studies into the psychological, neurological, genetic and cultural sources of delayed gratification. Theories sprung up in the fields of social psychology, medicine, political science, economics and even philosophy about the reasons why people might delay immediate gratification.

In purely Freudian terms, these children were struggling to control their "id" - which Freud suggested was the center of unconscious impulses. By extension, "idonomics" is the unleashing of the collective id on all of our social institutions -- from politics and economics, to religion and family life. My book _Idonomics_ explains, for example, how this operates in the worlds of business and the American consumer. With easy credit, looser regulations and lots of tempting offers, one might sympathize with the young couple who take advantage of the no-money-down, zero-income offers to buy a house or a car. Or why a homeowner might jump at the chance to refinance her home with a cash-out deal to upgrade her kitchen.

While it's easy to ignore the consequences of a million individual economic decisions, they can add up to one great big systemic risk, as we discovered during the 2008 financial meltdown that precipitated the Great Recession. While the average person may be only taking a small risk, the big players are often taking gigantic risks. Idonomics is when people simply abandon common sense in pursuit of the pleasure principle, and we all end up suffering as a result. Whether it's politicians grasping for short-term fixes while ignoring long-term problems, media companies sacrificing truth for ratings, or even religions offering wealth, health and happiness through prayer, our reckless pursuit of the pleasure principle has brought us to this mess.

The answer may not be to embrace French or Chinese parenting techniques, but as a society we need to examine our helter skelter approach to the American dream. By sacrificing long-term happiness for short-term pleasure, we have cheated ourselves and our children, and have endangered their legacy. The key to achieving and sustaining the American dream is not so simple as greater discipline, or Puritanical self-control, but rather in recognizing the difference between instant gratification and genuine fulfillment.

The MPAA Dinosaur and the SOPA Debacle

February 2012

The recent dust-up between the Hollywood studios and Internet companies reveals how out of touch Hollywood has become with its own customers. The idea of punishing consumers for ignoring Hollywood's business model is a futile strategy, as the music companies have learned over the past decade.

As Chris Anderson points out in his book *Free*, any product or service that can be delivered digitally will ultimately be available for free, or close to it. But that doesn't mean Hollywood movies have no value, it simply means that old Hollywood has to transform its business model -- along with newspapers, the music industry and virtually all other sectors of the economy.

One startling observation in Anderson's book is that Hollywood might even increase its profits by offering more of its products for free or nearly free. China is a case in point. For years, Hollywood has been trying to stamp out piracy in China, with little success. But what has actually happened is that widespread piracy has actually increased the appetite for movies in that nation of a billion people. As a Chinese middle class has emerged, consumers in China are buying more DVDs and other Hollywood products than ever, since they recognize the superior quality -- and even the status value -- of legitimately branded products. (Authentic Apple 4GS phones are now selling at three times retail price in China, when they are available).

So why does Hollywood continue its futile quest to protect an outdated business model, even when that strategy jeopardizes its long-term future? The answer is that the Hollywood lobbying effort is directed by a dinosaur-like organization called the Motion Picture Association of America (MPAA), which does not represent Hollywood at all, but only the narrow interests of its six member studios. Some of the most important filmmakers and film companies in America -- including Steven Spielberg and the Weinstein Company, Lions Gate and a host others -- have no say in the MPAA's direction or policy.

To say that the MPAA and its members are living in the past is an understatement. With the digital revolution and globalization of culture, the Hollywood studios can no longer completely dominate the global film market. In many countries, at least 50 percent of movies are locally made, and international co-productions are much more common. Still, the MPAA and the big six studios act as if they can dictate to the world market, and rather than adjusting their business practices to new market conditions. In fact, MPAA Chairman Chris Dodd is quoted as threatening to cut off "support" from politicians who don't tow the MPAA line.

Instead of trying to shut down popular websites and punish their opponents -- and their own customers -- Hollywood should take an entirely different approach to the digital revolution. And that should begin with forming a truly representative organization to promote Hollywood films. Ideally, the United States should have a National Film Commission that would represent not just the big studios, but also independent producers and filmmakers, along with labor unions, theater owners and distributors.

Virtually all nations except the United States have film commissions, which not only promote their film industries, but also provide a global network for filmmakers to create and promote their films. These need not be governmental organizations -- they are often a combination of public and private entities -- but they do serve the interests of each country in the global marketplace. Since Hollywood has never needed help before, a national film commission was never considered necessary.

But now that Hollywood is facing twin threats from the digital revolution and the growth of homegrown films in many major markets, it should join the international film community and form a national organization to meet the challenges of the new century. It is long past time when an elite and outmoded organization like the MPAA should be left to make policy for the entire American film industry.

Why the Big Banks Won't Change (Until We Change Them)

November 2011

You would think that a wholesale customer revolt against the big banks, including Bank of America, Chase and the others, might wake them up to the error of their ways in soaking their depositors with fees for everything from checking accounts to ATMs. But bank transfer protests and demonstrations outside branches unfortunately will do little to shake them up.

The fundamental reason is the bottom line. The big banks no longer rely on customer deposits or lending to make money. Despite a $700 billion bailout of the banks (or some would argue because of it), the banks still don't lend very much money to individuals or companies, at least not in America. For the big banks -- as well as the investment bankers like Goldman Sachs -- the real money is in arbitrage and sophisticated securities, like the infamous mortgage securities and credit default swaps that drenched the global economy with trillions in debt.

For all the protestations of their CEOs before Congress and elsewhere, the bankers have essentially abandoned America for greener pastures. After all, there is a lot more money to be made in emerging economies that are less regulated, have cheaper labor and are more easily corrupted or duped than American companies or workers, or even the American government. Why should they invest in America, the bankers say, when they can expect piddling returns for an equal amount of risk?

Despite the argument of the Republicans in Congress, this has very little to do with government regulation, and a lot more to do with the globalization of economics. The United States could wipe out every environmental and safety regulation on the books, outlaw organized labor and allow child labor, and the bankers would still prefer to put their money overseas. That's because Americans are not going to go back to the 19th century standards of living that included sweatshop conditions, child labor and gross environmental damage. On the other hand, many of the emerging nations are still willing -- for the time being -- to endure those conditions. So that's where the big bankers will rush to put their money.

It's not just the emerging economies where the bankers are profiting. It's also in many of the developed countries where the big banks can use their privileged position to profit. For example, Goldman Sachs has perfected the art of using inside information and analysis to sell what Senator Carl Levin characterized as "crap" to their customers, while at the same time secretly making big bets against the own customers in the market. The result? They make money both ways. In any other universe, that would be a gross conflict of interest. In big banking, it's business as usual.

Why should the big banks care about the traditional banking business -- customer deposits and lending -- when they can reap huge profits from gaming a system that is rigged in their favor? One answer might be that they could get punished for it. Big fines, more regulation or, heaven forbid, jail terms for the crooks. But after driving the global economy into a ditch, the bankers were rewarded with a $700 billion bailout, big bonuses, and most importantly, a return to business as usual.

It is true that the $700 billion bailout was probably necessary to prevent a worldwide depression, but the big bonuses and return to business as usual was not. When the Bush and Obama administrations gave the big banks the bailout, the banks were expected to put the money back into the American economy. That never happened. Most of the money either still sits in the banks, or was invested in the risky profit engines that these banks still operate. Furthermore, there was virtually no new regulation of the riskiest operations of the banks, nor was there any real effort to punish the banks and bankers who profited from the global economic debacle, or to prevent them from doing it all over again.

We can protest all we want by changing our accounts to smaller banks or credit unions, but the big banks will continue along their merry way until the government reins them in. They don't make much money from America, so while the bankers may pay lip service to the concerns of ordinary Americans, they have no reason to care. The solution is simple: Force the banks to go back to traditional banking. If that means turning them into non-profits, so be it. But there is no way to justify allowing them to continue to bilk average American customers, not to mention risking driving the global economy off the cliff again.

The Promise of Obama's Second Term

October 2011

The prospects for President Obama's re-election have dimmed considerably in the past few months, but it is worth considering -- especially for his supporters -- what an Obama second term might look like. While the President's failings in the first term have been well chronicled, most recently in Ron Suskind's book *Confidence Men*, what are the chances for a different, more successful second term in the White House?

Although the economy will certainly seal Obama's fate, both in the election and in a second term, much will depend on the President himself. The rap on Obama during the campaign was that he was great at inspiring speeches but short on specific policies or experience. To a large extent, that criticism has been borne out by the events of his first term.

As described by Suskind and others, Obama has been a poor manager, often outmatched by advisers like Rahm Emmanuel and Larry Summers, who hijacked the domestic agenda and ran circles around the President in terms of implementing policy. Obama has also proven that while he doesn't exactly have a tin ear for politics, he certainly doesn't have the political acuity of a Bill Clinton or even a Ronald Reagan, both inside and outside the Beltway.

Having said that, Obama still has several things going for him. He is an inspiring speechmaker, better than either Reagan or Clinton, and possibly even FDR. While the Republicans like to blast his "empty rhetoric," Obama has an almost preternatural ability to lift his audiences to a loftier plain, especially on the knotty, divisive issues of our time. This alone can be a great gift of leadership if used properly.

And people still like him. Despite the plunge in his approval ratings and general pessimism about the country, the public likes Obama, even some of those who disagree with his policies. The criticisms of his performance as President are that he is weak, or that he has been mislead by his advisors or by powerful special interests. However, lots of people are still rooting for him to succeed. Compare this to the public view of George Bush, who was widely disliked at the end of his presidency, and even Bill Clinton, who people only grudgingly acknowledged was an effective leader despite his moral failings.

Assuming Obama overcomes the steep climb to re-election, what can he do differently in the second term? First of all, acknowledge his shortcomings -- at least to himself if not to the American public. After his historic election, Obama seemed determined to prove that he could excel at every aspect of the Presidency, despite his lack of experience. Obama is not a good manager and probably never will be. Instead of trying to fill that role, he should hire good people who have those skills and make them accountable. (Bill Daley as Chief of Staff was a first step in that direction).

Obama should also accept that his political instincts are far from perfect. Again, that does not present insurmountable problems, since there are lots of folks inside and outside the Beltway with highly tuned political instincts. He should hire them and listen to them. Axelrod, Plouffe and Jarrett are fine, but they are essentially loyalists -- other voices are needed for authentic balance.

If Obama is a poor manager with only middling political savvy, what does he have to offer America in a second term? The answer -- plenty. If he is re-elected, Obama still has the opportunity -- and it is a rare one for American presidents -- to be a transformational leader. In a very telling quote from Suskind's book, John Podesta, Clinton's Chief of Staff and head of Obama's transition team, describes what is probably Obama's greatest strength, and what separates him from brilliant political strategists like Clinton. "Obama draws people out of their comfort zone, " Podesta is quoted as saying. "He ends up making them rise to the occasion. He doesn't just synthesize and sell a solution. He's creating a space where solutions can happen."

In an era where America is undergoing a profound transformation in both its economic structure and its political culture, creating a national space for solutions may be the ultimate test of presidential leadership. Few presidents, with the exception perhaps of FDR and Lincoln, have had the opportunity, and challenge, to lead the nation through such an enormous transition. Any historian will acknowledge that it was neither strong managerial skills nor political instincts that made those leaders strong. Instead, it was their vision of America and its future that guided these presidents through years of failure and struggle. If Obama can develop a clear-eyed vision of America's future -- and of his own strengths and weaknesses as a leader -- then his second term holds great promise.

Can America Afford Equality?

September 2011

In his recent book, *Pinched*, about the Great Recession, author Don Peck points out that the top 1 percent of Americans possess as much wealth as the bottom 90 percent. In terms of income growth, two out of every three dollars in growth goes to the top 1 percent, while the other 99 percent share one lousy buck.

A 2005 report by Citigroup concluded that the future of the American economy did not depend on the much-vaunted American consumer, but rather rested on the spending and investments of the very wealthy. The Citigroup analysts called this a *plutonomy*, in which economic growth is powered by the wealthy few. The global economy, with its rapid rate of change and complexity, said the analysts, would be exploited primarily by the "rich and educated."

The Republicans in Congress have, in effect, endorsed this view of the future of the American economy by arguing that economic growth rests on tax cuts for the wealthy and large corporations, cutting expenditures on social programs for the poor and middle class, and reducing government regulation of businesses, including environmental and safety rules. All this fits nicely into an economic view of America as two separate groups -- the rich and the rest of us.

Conservatives argue that subsidizing the rich and large multinational corporations, along with cutting government spending, will create jobs. The question, however, is what jobs and for whom? While the high-tech and financial industries clustered in places like Seattle, San Francisco, Boston and New York have quickly rebounded with high-paying jobs for the educated elite, entrepreneurs and Fortune 500 executives, jobs for the middle-class are rapidly disappearing, and there is little prospect that simply improving the lot of the rich and highly educated will help the vast majority of Americans to find a decent job.

Even if one concedes the argument (which I for one do not) that most of the future growth will come from the richest 1 percent of Americans and the handful of multinational corporations, is it really in the interest of America to wander down that primrose path? Throughout recent history, virtually every society that has ignored the fundamental principle of equality has run into serious trouble. A stroll through the leafy streets of an upper-class enclave in South America or the high walls of a Middle Eastern compound for the wealthy -- all equipped with machine-toting guards and high-tech surveillance cameras -- should convince anyone that, despite the economic benefits of a *plutonomy*, the social price is too great for any nation to endure.

America has always been -- and still remains -- dedicated to the principle of equality, even though (or perhaps because) many of its citizens had to overcome centuries of injustice and oppression. Equality of opportunity and equal treatment under the law are foundations of American society. These principles are not mere abstractions -- they have been critical to the tremendous success of the American economy over the past two hundred and thirty-five years. From small businesses to farmers, from steel workers to janitors, America represents the dream of a better life, based on equality of opportunity. While the odds are often long, and the dream is fading, there remains the hope that, with hard work and passion, success is still possible in America.

However, if we as Americans accept the idea that the only hope for our future rests with the rich and the multinationals, and that we must abandon the fundamental principle of equality of opportunity, then perhaps we need to take another look at the American Dream. Even if it is not strictly in our economic interest, don't we have an obligation to the "bottom 90 percent" of American society who are so easily dismissed as irrelevant to future economic growth? Do we really want to live in a country with a slightly higher GDP, but where 90 percent of the people live in stagnation or worse? And what would be the social consequences of abandoning our commitment to equality and tossing the American Dream overboard?

As President Obama pointed out in his speech to Congress recently, that is not the kind of America any of us want. It is certainly true that the American economy -- along with the global economy -- is in the midst of a deep crisis. There is great suffering as people lose their jobs, their houses and their future. And we must do everything we can to find jobs for the jobless and homes for the homeless. But we cannot forget our deep devotion to the principles that America was founded upon, and must not sacrifice our commitment to equality in the face of this crisis.

We Don't Need an "Obama Doctrine"

August 2011

There has been a lot of fuss in the past several weeks about the lack of a coherent "Obama doctrine" in foreign policy. Critics and commentators have been dissecting his past speeches and pronouncements, searching for a coherent "doctrine" to support his foreign policy approach to events in Libya and elsewhere. Conservatives and liberals alike have been criticizing Obama for moving too slowly or too fast, for failing to act unilaterally, or for too embracing the military option too quickly.

Why, they ask, is the United States intervening in support of the Libyan rebellion, yet failing to assert its influence when protesters are being shot in Bahrain or in Syria? What is the explanation for humanitarian intervention in some cases and not others? Why do we continue to support some repressive regimes and actively oppose others? Have we abandoned our leadership role in the world? Or, as others say, have we not learned the lessons of other failed military interventions?

What both sides of this argument are looking for is a steadfast statement of principles that can be applied to American foreign policy. They want an "Obama doctrine" that sends a clear message to the world about America's approach to international relations, a blanket declaration of "we shall" or "we shall not." However, the simple truth is that we don't need an "Obama doctrine." Perhaps we needed a "Nixon doctrine" or even a "Bush doctrine," but the last thing we need in these uncertain times is a doctrinaire approach to the world.

The criticism of leaders, especially American leaders, who take a pragmatic, case-by-case view of foreign policy is that they are pursuing a strategy of "realpolitik," the phrase coined by German writer Ludwig Von Roschau to describe the nineteenth-century machinations of Otto von Bismark in unifying Prussia and Count Metternich in carving up Europe at the Congress of Vienna. More recently, Henry Kissinger was accused of practicing "realpolitik" in the diplomatic overtures to China and in the handling of the Arab-Israeli conflict.

Much of the negative connotations of "realpolitik" come from traditional American suspicion of the Machiavellian character of European politics and the horrific conflicts that were in part the result of flawed statesmanship. However, "realpolitik" is really nothing more than a practical view of the relations between nations. The United States, like every other country, must take into account several factors in dealing with the rest of the world and with conflicts that inevitably arise. First, what is our national interest and how is it impacted? Secondly, what are the principles that are important to us as a nation and how are they being threatened? Finally, what role can we play in each particular case?

There is little question that, throughout history, American leadership has generally weighed the first two factors in our foreign policy. From the Monroe doctrine to the Bush doctrine, there has always been considerable weight given to America's national interest and our guiding principles. The real question today is a more pragmatic one -- what role can we play in each specific case?

For much of the post-World War Two era, the answer to that question was fairly simple. Up until the collapse of the Soviet Union, our role was to be a counterbalance to the nuclear-armed and often aggressive Soviet empire. But after the end of the Cold War, America was thrust into the unprecedented position of being the indisputable world leader in terms of military, political and economic power. When a political or humanitarian crisis sprung up anywhere in the world, the United States was the first on call and also the last resort.

After 9/11, the rise of China's economic power and the advent of a global marketplace, America was no longer in the same position. While we still have by far the greatest military might, our economic and political clout has been diminished. We were no longer in a position to dictate an American "doctrine" to the rest of the world, as George Bush discovered when he enunciated the "Bush doctrine," which was viewed almost universally as a case of American overreaching.

If the Obama presidency stands for anything, it is that an ideological or doctrinaire approach to difficult problems, whether internationally or domestically, will not work. This is not a matter of Barack Obama's temperament, or the politics of the country, but rather because of America's changed position in the world. We must take a "realpolitik" approach to foreign policy because we have no other choice. There is no "Obama doctrine" that we can apply as a general principle when there is so much uncertainty in the world.

It would be foolish to promote a doctrine that encouraged either intervention or isolation as a general rule. There are no easy answers to challenges that we face in Libya and elsewhere in the Middle East, not to mention the wars in Afghanistan and Iraq, or our relationship with China. To push for an overriding, simplistic doctrine would be foolhardy, and flies in the face of the current reality of our world and America's role in it.

Is It Time for a National Film Commission?

August 2011

With the Toronto Film Festival going on, it's worth pointing out the crucial role that national film commissions like Canada's National Film Board and Telefilm Canada have played in the global film marketplace. These agencies of the Canadian government not only assist filmmakers in the production of their films, but also help global marketing, distribution and promotion of Canadian films in general. The result has been a boon for Canadian filmmakers and an important source of revenue for Canada.

Like Canada, most nations recognize that films are a valuable export and that, in a competitive global marketplace, filmmakers need help in marketing and distributing films outside their own countries. In addition, with the growth of international co-productions, filmmakers need assistance from their national film commissions - who are part of an international network -- to provide information to facilitate those partnerships.

Since national film commissions are pretty inexpensive to operate and can reap huge economic benefits for a country, virtually every developed nation, and many in the developing world, operate these commissions. However, there is one nation - the only one in the Western world -- that does not have a national film commission. Guess who? The United States.

There are lots of reasons for this glaring omission, but let's start with the obvious one -- we have never needed a national film commission. Since Hollywood has always been (and continues to be) the dominant player in the international film market, it never needed any help. The Hollywood studios had their own international network, and didn't see any reason to for a national film commission. In fact, it was in their interest to discourage such an effort, since it might to undermine the clout of the studios.

While we don't have a national film commission, we do have a de facto arbiter of rules and standards -- The Motion Picture Association of America, the industry association of the six major movie studios. Founded in 1922 by the early movie moguls, the MPAA is the single most powerful voice for American films and has played a key role in the global success of American cinema. Jack Valenti, the former aide to LBJ who ran the MPAA for nearly forty years, was a skilled and passionate advocate for Hollywood, championing the movie industry and crafting a ratings system that the public could rely on.

During Valenti's tenure, the movie business changed radically from a mostly domestic industry dependent on US theatrical revenues into a global business that relies on foreign ticket sales and a multitude of technologies and distribution platforms. However, the structure of the MPAA has changed little, and consists of only six members -- Disney, Fox, Universal, Paramount, Sony and Warner Brothers. With the exception of Disney, all of these studios have become subsidiaries of larger media conglomerates. And many of the most important film companies and filmmakers in America (including DreamWorks and Steven Spielberg) -- not to mention theater owners and other industry groups -- are not members of the MPAA and have no voice in its activities. While the MPAA never set out to be a representative organization -- it has always operated essentially as an industry cartel -- the changing nature of the global film business raises questions about the effectiveness of the MPAA as the chief promoter of American films.

There are two important forces driving the global film market today. The first is the advent of digital and internet technologies that are changing how films are produced, distributed and consumed. These new technologies have offered opportunities for Hollywood -- for example, many more distribution platforms -- as well as challenges, including widespread film piracy. In addition, the explosive growth of countries like China, India, Russia and Brazil -- to name only a few -- has increased worldwide audiences for film, but also threatens to change future viewing habits, as global audiences look for new stories that reflect their own experiences and cultures.

Industry organizations like the MPAA are simply not up to these challenges. While it may be an effective lobbying organization for the studios, it has focused primarily on anti-piracy efforts and the ratings system, but has done little to address the broader challenges of the global market. This is due, in large part, to competing interests among the members of the MPAA, who are huge conglomerates that can rarely agree on a broad agenda.

The best vehicle to address the challenges of the global market would be a national film commission -- a public/private organization that would include representatives of both the film industry and the federal government. While it would be politically difficult to establish a strictly governmental body, a compromise solution might be a private/public partnership that would enlist the power of the United States government in the global market without limiting the freedom of the film industry.

The American film industry is one of our most important engines of economic growth and, during these tough economic times and in the face of a rapidly changing global marketplace, it does not make sense to rely on a small group of tradition-bound studios to lead the industry into the future. Only a private/public partnership that reflects a broader swath of the film community is capable of maintaining this critical source of jobs and revenue.

Although the Hollywood studios, networks, unions and other organizations might resist the idea of a national film commission, it is arguably in their long-term interest to have a more representative organization in place. Perhaps most importantly, a national film commission could have a positive impact on the creative potential of the American film community by connecting it more directly to other national film commissions and thereby to the global marketplace. Now is the time for America to take this crucial step towards the future.

"Idonomics" and the American Dream

May 2011

In the late 1960s, at a nursery school on the campus of Stanford University, Walter Mischel, an Austrian-born psychologist, began an experiment involving four-year-olds and marshmallows. He offered the children a tempting choice -- they could have one marshmallow right away, or if they waited a few minutes, they could have two marshmallows. The kids struggled mightily, trying to avoid eating the delicious treat right away, but only about thirty percent were able to delay gratification even for a few minutes. Mischel's experiments spawned a whole range of studies into the mechanics of delayed gratification. No matter where these studies led -- and they were often inconclusive -- they always returned to a fundamental question for human beings -- do we eat the marshmallow now or later? Do we postpone immediate pleasure for some future reward? Do we embrace the pleasure principle or do we override it -- either in the name of some overarching principle or simply because it will benefit us to wait?

Sigmund Freud was one of the first modern thinkers to tackle this question in his structural model of the human psyche. In Freud's view, the id is a fundamental component of our personality that works to satisfy our basic urges, needs and desires. Freud's id was based on the pleasure principle, which says that people will seek pleasure and avoid pain in order to meet their biological and psychological needs. The id doesn't care about reality or the needs of others. It seeks only its own satisfaction. Over the past fifty years, the pleasure principle -- the id -- has dominated American society. From the "me" generation of the 1970s to the wretched excesses of the 2000s, there has been a disturbing shift in American values from community responsibility to individual gratification, from long-term investment to short-term profit, from self-sacrifice to instant reward. The result has been "idonomics" -- in which the pleasure principle dominates not only the marketplace, but also our politics, media, technology and even our personal relationships.

It's pretty easy to see how idonomics operates in the economic sphere. Executives pump up their stock price even as their companies are at risk. Or the young couple signs up for a no-money-down, zero-income offer to buy a house or a car. It's easy to ignore the consequences of a million individual economic decisions until they add up to one great big systemic risk, as we discovered during the 2008 financial meltdown that precipitated the Great Recession. It's not only in the economic sphere that idonomics wreaks havoc. Federal budget deficits have skyrocketed as politicians promised voters the pleasures of generous government programs without the pain of paying for them -- a textbook example of idonomics in action.

In health care, we've been practicing idonomics instead of good medicine as drug companies spend millions of dollars on researching new drugs to treat impotence, weight loss and aging while ignoring drugs used to cure deadly illnesses. In the media world, idonomics meant the pursuit of short-term profit at the expense of long-term quality. In technology, money goes to speculative investment and new consumer devices rather than to solving the energy crisis or improving infrastructure.

Idonomics has even infected our cultural values and personal relationships. Looking at America today, you see a decline in our time-honored values of responsibility, respect and a concern for others. How often do you see a young man offer his seat on the bus to an old lady or pregnant woman? What about the woman chatting loudly on her cell phone in the supermarket? While these may seem like small matters, they are indicative of a much bigger trend in our society -- the arrival of cultural idonomics. This "me first" attitude has also impacted our personal relationships. Since the 1980s, the divorce rate has tripled in most Western countries, including the United States. Marriage, like all personal relationships, requires hard work and an investment in the future. It requires deferred gratification and self-sacrifice, and neither has a place in idonomics.

Unfortunately, it is not easy to undo the damage of idonomics. Willpower alone -- saying "no" to the pursuit of pleasure -- certainly won't work. However, research by Mischel and others suggest that there are techniques that humans can use to defer immediate gratification. The four-year-olds in his study who avoided focusing on the marshmallows by covering their eyes or singing songs were able to hold off. Another technique was "peer modeling," in which children who were shown a video of a child using distraction techniques were able to successfully delay gratification. While overcoming the societal dynamic of idonomics is a tougher challenge, the Great Recession has provided a powerful opportunity for our society to change course. Profound lessons about risk and the unbridled pursuit of pleasure often make a lasting imprint. But we must be continually reminded of those lessons, which we can too easily forget.

For fifty years, the American Dream has been jeopardized by the unrestrained pursuit of the pleasure principle. Can the American Dream survive idonomics? Absolutely. We don't need to embrace a new Puritanism or extreme self-sacrifice. With a combination of traditional American values of common sense, along with newer research techniques for promoting deferred gratification, we can certainly get back on the right path. If we think of idonomics as the fevered frenzy of the past, and begin to build our economy, our institutions and even our families on a more solid, practical foundation, we can overcome the excesses of the past and return the American Dream to its rightful place.

Libya: Fighting the Last War

March 2011

If there is one thing that is certain about recent events in the Middle East, it is uncertainty. Who would have predicted six months ago that the immolation of a college-educated street peddler in a rural Tunisian town would lead to the fall of the regimes in Tunisia and Egypt, the descent of Libya into civil war and widespread unrest against autocratic regimes throughout the region?

The broad impact of social media, as well as television outlets like Al-Jazeera and Al-Arabiya, has radically altered the political and social landscape of the Middle East. For Arab governments -- governments that face a vast array of different challenges in each of their societies -- this has meant a rapid and even desperate re-examination of their approach to governing. Who would have imagined six months ago that the Syrian government would talking about reform or that the rulers of Bahrain would be calling in troops from Saudi Arabia?

All this fast-paced change has also meant some serious re-examination by the international community, including the United States. France, for example, which sat out the Iraq war and embraced Qaddafi until recently, has taken the aggressive lead in attacking the Libyan regime. Meanwhile, the Obama administration, mindful of the errors of the Iraq invasion and subsequent quagmire, has taken a very cautious approach to intervention.

But Obama's critics in the United States don't seem to have taken full measure of the rapid changes in the Middle East. Republican leaders like John McCain and Newt Gingrich pressed President Obama for an early and aggressive military intervention, apparently dismissing the sensitive political and diplomatic issues in the region, as well as the missteps of the Iraq war. Clearly, theirs was a case of rigid thinking and an unwillingness to carefully examine a fluid, volatile situation. In short, a knee-jerk reaction based on fixed ideas and doctrine.

However, it wasn't only the Republicans who had a knee-jerk reaction. There are also many on the left who seem to be looking in the rear-view mirror at the Iraq experience, even when the Obama administration was displaying deliberative caution, a collaborative international approach and a strong sensitivity to the image of America in the region. While there is great uncertainty in this military and political intervention, the lesson going forward must be one of flexibility, collaboration and caution -- traits that were decidedly missing in the Bush administration's foreign policy.

There is an old saying that "Generals are always fighting the last war" -- developing strategy and tactics for whatever battle they recently fought. This is also true in politics and diplomacy, where governments and their leaders develop fixed ideas about every conflict so that the question becomes "How do we fit this situation into our familiar box of ideas?" In fact, the Middle East today ought to be a prime case of thinking outside of the box. There is not going to be a one-size-fits-all solution, either militarily or politically. And the solution that works today may not work tomorrow, or the next day.

President Obama has been criticized from both the right and the left for his Libya policy over the past few weeks. And those critics may turn out to be correct. However, considering the uncertain and fluid nature of the crisis, Obama's policy approach has been fundamentally sound. Many have argued that his cautious style is too timid or unduly moderate. But a steady, deliberative hand is arguably the most effective approach to leadership in uncertain times. What is certain is that old thinking -- fighting the last war -- will not work in an era of rapid change.

Who Needs The Government?

February 2011

The raging debate between Democrats and Republicans over government spending and taxation touches on fundamental questions about the rationale for government, questions that go back as far as Plato's *Republic*. The biggest hue and cry is coming from the Tea Partiers, whose views range from traditional small government advocates to extreme libertarians. But the debate raises the question for all Americans -- "Who needs the government?"

Most of us would agree that we all need the government to provide basic services -- public safety, infrastructure and national defense. But even those basic services are fairly recent additions to the government's role. In the nineteenth century, for example, most fire departments were private, paid for by insurance companies. If you paid a premium to the insurance company, the fire department would put out a fire at your house. If you did not pay a premium, your house burned down. In 1883, in Riverside, California, a major commercial building burned down, but the city fathers refused to pay $500 for a municipal fire department, arguing there was no need for one. Finally, in 1887, after another disastrous fire, the city's first public fire department was established.

Times have changed, and virtually all Americans agree that government has a role to play in providing essential public services. The question then becomes, what is essential? Is it "essential" that we provide a social safety net for the old, the infirm, the disabled and the poor? If a building burns down in the middle of town, the consequences are obvious and it's clear something has to be done. But what about public health, education, the environment or infrastructure? Are those really essential? Many in the Tea Party believe that some or all of these are not essential public services, at least not in their current form. Even moderate Republicans are calling for large cutbacks in these services.

In an ideal world, we could sit down together and have an "adult" conversation about what public services we need and how much we should spend. Instead of having an abstract, ideological debate about the merits of taxation versus spending, we could develop a consensus, set priorities and find solutions. In that case, everyone would have to give up a little -- or even a lot. However, this is not an ideal world, and politics usually trumps adult conversations every time. Americans from all sides have vested interests in the outcome of this national conversation, often based on issues that transcend spending or taxation, with a greater emphasis on values (and emotions) than practical solutions.

Speaking of values, now would be a good time to examine more deeply our fundamental American values. If we can agree that liberty, justice and equality of opportunity are bedrock American values, what is the role of government in preserving our values? We have fought a revolution and civil war for these values, and the goal of those struggles was to establish and defend a government that would preserve those values. We did not fight for a bigger government or a smaller government, or even for higher or lower taxes (the Boston Tea Party, remember, was about representation, not just taxation). What we fought for was to protect our fundamental values.

So what role does government play in protecting those values? Above all, the government is the instrument of our democracy. It is the organization that the American people have created to represent and promote the values that we hold sacred. Unlike in many other countries, we have been given the right to determine the shape and direction of that government. Of course, there are lots of special interests and frustrating bureaucracies that are obstacles in our path, but ultimately, we have the power to decide. Perhaps more importantly, we have very few fundamental barriers to exercising that power. We don't have to belong to a particular religion or privileged group, and we don't have to be members of any party or organization. All we have to do is make our voices heard.

In many respects, the government is the embodiment of some of our highest aspirations as Americans. Rather than being a rowdy collection of individuals, or even a rough coalition of states, we look to the federal government, and to a lesser extent state and local governments, to embody a collective vision of America. In our highly individualistic and competitive society, we look to government to regulate individual actions and responsibilities for the sake of the greater good. No one else but the government -- not the corporation, or the church or even the family -- can protect the larger interests of our society.

As President Obama recently said, "We are the government." It makes no sense to be anti-government in the American context, unless you are opposed to the values that it represents. If, for example, you believe in state ownership of all private enterprises, you would probably oppose the government. Or, if you believe that the best government is no government at all, then you would also oppose our system. But, short of that, you really ought to be rooting for the best government we can muster.

That doesn't mean that the government shouldn't change and improve -- it should. It also doesn't mean that there is one, simple solution to complex problems. For example, solving the government deficit isn't just a matter of either raising taxes or cutting budgets. As every family knows, the key to financial solvency is the judicious balancing of income and expenditures -- which depends on the priorities that each family sets. And that bring us back to values. In these contentious and uncertain times, we have to keep our eyes on the prize -- our fundamental values of liberty, justice and equality of opportunity. We can disagree of the path to insuring those values, and the degree to which government plays a role in our lives. But, as Americans, we should never forget the enduring values that have made us a great nation and that bind us together.

Closing the "Open Carry" Loophole

February 2011

What would you do if you walked into a downtown McDonald's and were confronted with a group of men carrying guns? If you are like most of us, you would probably flee for your life and then immediately call the cops. However, in California and many other states, there is not much the police could do except keep a close eye on the armed men.

While some states ban the practice of "open carry" of weapons, most states permit the open carrying of firearms, often with few or no restrictions. Ironically, some of the Southern states like Texas, Oklahoma, Arkansas and South Carolina ban open carrying of weapons - a vestige of the post-Civil War Reconstruction era. However, in the wake of the Tucson shootings, efforts have begun to repeal "open carry" laws that have been exploited for political purposes by the more extreme elements of the gun rights community.

In California, Assemblyman Anthony Portantino has introduced a bill that would repeal the "open carry" loophole in state law. The bill, which is supported by police organizations, has also been introduced in similar form in the Los Angeles City Council. Although a repeal bill was introduced in the California Assembly in 2010, it died because of opposition from gun rights activists. However, Portantino and other supporters hope that recent events, including several shootings at Los Angeles schools, will tip the balance toward repeal.

It is worth noting that the "open carry" movement, which featured visits by gun-toting men to Starbucks, is controversial even within the gun rights movement. Charles Cotton, a prominent gun rights activist and NRA Board Member, wrote on his blog, "The open-carry issue has pitted gun owners against one another like no other issue. Even the so-called 'assault weapons' ban didn't generate so much hostility between friends." Cotton, who believes that the open-carry movement will "damage our ability to promote the interest of gun owners in the future," points out that the NRA has not taken a position on open-carry legislation in Texas, which would lift the ban on carrying weapons openly in public.

Ironically, the first legislation in California to restrict public carrying of firearms came in 1967 in response to members of the Black Panther party openly carrying guns, notably in front of the State Capitol. This prompted the passage of the Mulford Act, which prohibited the public carrying of loaded firearms. The bill was signed into law by none other than Governor Ronald Reagan. In that case - as in the case of the "open carry" movement in the Starbucks stores - the legislation was prompted by provocative displays of firearms aimed at making a political point.

There is simply no rationale for the open carrying of weapons, an act which itself can be viewed as a provocation. Even arch-conservative Supreme Court Justice Scalia has written that "Like most rights, the Second Amendment right is not unlimited. It is not a right to keep and carry any weapon whatsoever in any manner whatsoever and for whatever purpose."

Some gun rights advocates have argued that the Tucson shooter might have been stopped if one of the bystanders were carrying a gun. In fact, it was reported that there was an onlooker who had a licensed gun. Interviewed after the shootings, the onlooker admitted that, in the confusion of the moment, he had very nearly shot the wrong man - one of the heroes who had wrestled the shooter to the ground. So much for the wisdom of more guns on the scene.

As the son and grandson of career Army officers and one who grew up with guns - I got my first .22 when I was twelve years old and hunted often with my grandfather - I cannot begin to see the rationale for permitting the open carrying of guns in public. I cannot imagine that my father and grandfather - who had witnessed the horrors of weaponry up close - would ever have supported publicly introducing weapons carried openly by civilians in a public place. It is a recipe for mayhem and should be banned once and for all.

The Pathos of Sarah Palin

January 2011

In what will hopefully be her political "last hurrah" as a presidential contender, Sarah Palin has revealed her small-minded approach to leadership. In a time of national mourning, Palin has seen only the attacks on her own image rather than the larger, more complex issues that the assassinations in Tucson raise. Her defensive remarks seem more like the spitefulness of a third-grader who last year got the most Valentines but this year got none than the reflections of a national leader.

In the wake of all our national tragedies - from the assassination of political figures to the attacks on 9/11 -- the nation has gone through substantial soul-searching, and finger-pointing, in an effort to absorb our grief. It is a time for national leaders to urge restraint, prayer and humility, rather than ideology or politics. In her speech, Sarah Palin turned every decent notion of leadership on its head and used the Tucson tragedy as a moment to defend herself politically.

Her empty prattle about individual responsibility and First Amendment rights bears no relation to the events in Tucson or her role as a political leader. It is simply absurd to link the right to freedom of speech with her responsibilities as a national figure. As a citizen, Palin can say anything she wants to, but is it wise for a political leader even to tiptoe, however gently, towards the bright line of advocating violence? And how can a politician who has benefited so much from media attention now complain that the media has committed "blood libel" by exploring the connection between extreme rhetoric and violence?

The juvenile narcissism and unbridled political ambition of Sarah Palin has shown itself to have no boundaries. Fortunately for our country, she also has a real self-destructive streak, which is evidenced by her ill-conceived and ill-timed remarks. The greatest threat to Palin is not from her critics in the media and on the left, but from herself. In any case, she has greatly diminished her standing by her behavior at a time of national crisis.

Obama's Story

January 2011

Creative writers and artists who spend their lives crafting narratives have long understood that we do not so much create a story as discover it. As Michelangelo said, "In every block of marble I see a statue as plain as though it stood before me. I have only to hew away the rough walls that imprison the lovely apparition."

The narrative of politics is not very different, as President Obama has demonstrated over the last month. For the past two years, as he struggled to restore jobs to the economy, pass health care and fulfill other lofty campaign promises, he was roundly criticized for failing to communicate effectively with the American people. While the White House insisted they had a good story to tell, they conceded that they had done a poor job of telling it.

However, both the White House and its critics were wrong. The failure was not in communicating the story the administration wanted to tell, but in revealing the story that was unfolding on the American political stage. As any writer will tell you, the most important character in any story is the audience or reader. In the narrative of American politics, that is the public.

Beginning with the deadlocked Bush-Gore election of 2000, the American people have been yearning for a new narrative, a transformative story that will release us from the prison of partisanship and deadlock, and inspire us to remake the American dream. During the 2008 campaign, Obama's personal story was the touchstone for this new narrative -- a nation that could elect an African-American president after a legacy of slavery and oppression would surely be an inspiration for the future. Even more profoundly, the vision of an America uniting for change, overcoming the mistakes and bitterness of the past, and reconciling for a renewed destiny created a powerful story.

But the narrative grew cloudy after the campaign ended and the grind of governing began. The recession threw the economy -- and the administration -- into a ditch. Health care reform became a messy slog and the war in Afghanistan looked like a quagmire. Where was the transformative change that Obama promised? Was the story he told during the campaign mere fantasy? Or even worse, was it nothing but a political tall tale?

Ironically, the "shellacking" of the Democrats in the midterm elections has provided the answer to those questions. The midterm message from the public was crystal clear -- "We want progress, not partisanship." It was a good, strong dose of common sense from the electorate, rejecting ideological extremes in favor of unified, bipartisan action to solve our nation's pressing problems. Responsible leaders on both sides of the aisle recognize that the American people will simply not tolerate the deadlock and partisanship of the past decade. We need to confront our problems and begin to solve them, together.

During the campaign, Barack Obama was criticized for repeating the quote from the poet June Jordan, who, in referring to South African women, wrote, "We are the ones we have been waiting for." For his critics, the line seemed like empty rhetorical nonsense. However, the midterm message from the voters makes the quote seem quite prescient. Once again, the voters have spoken loud and clear, not only to President Obama, but to the leaders of both parties. We, the American people, have delivered the message that we have been waiting for.

Storytellers know that our greatest gift is not in creating a story, but in revealing it by listening and observing. Only then will our stories truly reflect the human experience and thus resonant with audiences and readers. Over the past month, President Obama and our leaders in Congress, with the tax cut compromise, the passage of the new Start Treaty and the repeal of "Don't ask, don't tell" are showing us that they have started listening, and a new narrative has begun to emerge. Like Michelangelo discovering the statute in the block of marble, I hope that our political leaders will continue to listen and discover the story that is emerging from the many voices of America. It is a story worth telling.

The Tax Cut Deal: Beating the Republicans at Their Own Game

December 2010

At first blush, President Obama's tax cut deal -- trading an extension of tax cuts for the wealthy in return for an extension of unemployment benefits for millions of Americans -- is a setback for Obama and the Democrats. But a closer look at the reality of the deal makes this a clear win for Obama, and probably for Democrats in the long run. Even better, it appears that Obama has finally hit his stride and is now beating the Republicans at their own game.

Granted, it is outrageous to be subsidizing tax breaks for millionaires in the midst of the Great Recession -- not to mention adding to the deficit. But let's look at the facts for a moment -- both of the policy and the politics. First, on the policy front, the tax cut deal amounts to a $900 billion dollar stimulus package at a time when most economists -- notably progressive economists like Paul Krugman -- are calling for continued stimulus to promote economic growth. Can you imagine the reaction from the Republicans and the Tea Partiers -- not to mention Blue Dog Democrats -- if Obama had proposed a $900 billion stimulus package? But that is exactly what the Republicans have agreed to.

This was clearly a case where the White House outfoxed the Republicans by leveraging their own inconsistent ideology against them. At the very same time that the Republicans are screaming about government spending and about lowering the deficit, they were stonewalling any attempt to take away big tax handouts to the wealthiest Americans. Okay, said Obama, have it your way. We'll let you have your tax cut extension in return for extending assistance to the millions of unemployed Americans who desperately need our help. Fine, said the Republicans, perhaps gloating over their tax cut victory, but not realizing that theirs was nothing more than a Pyrrhic victory. The net result -- another $900 billion stimulus package. Try explaining that to the Tea Partiers.

When you look at the politics of the deal, Obama's victory over the Republicans seems even more impressive. Another $900 billion in stimulus funds will certainly help to hasten the recovery, which is already on a slow uptick. By 2012, the economy should be on the upswing, if not in full recovery, which will only help Obama's re-election prospects. Clearly, the single most important factor in the re-election of any presidential incumbent is the state of the economy, and this week's tax cut deal makes Obama's re-election chances look considerably brighter. (For the sake of the country, we must address the deficit for the long term. But I would much rather have rational, progressive approach to deficit cutting than the knee-jerk, inconsistent Tea Party sloganeering).

As for the Republicans, the tax cut deal rips open the inconsistencies in both their politics and their policies. From a policy standpoint, they are screaming about the deficit and government spending while they push for tax cuts for the richest Americans at the expense of millions of the unemployed. In any universe, that is both bad politics and bad policy. Their position will come back to haunt them as they try to explain their position not only to the Republican base, but especially to independents in the future.

Perhaps more importantly -- from the perspective of political optics -- the public will recognize before long that the Republicans cut a very bad deal, and that Obama was particularly adroit in outmaneuvering them. In fact, this deal may be the same kind of important turning point as the Gingrich shutdown of the government in 1995. Looking back, the tax cut deal may be regarded as the point when Obama finally regained his stride.

From a purely political perspective, the opposition that Obama is experiencing from Democrats in Congress is actually a positive for the White House. When the rest of the country -- especially the independents -- see Obama getting flack from his own party for the deal, he will rise in their estimation as someone who is willing to take on his own base. In truth, when the outlines of this Obama victory become clear, it is likely that most Democrats in Congress and around the country will realize that Obama has regained his mojo and outfoxed the Republicans at their own game.

Losing the Battle, But Winning the War

November 2010

The latest figures on wealth distribution are nothing less than shocking. The top one percent of Americans now control about 35% of the total economic wealth of the nation and the top 10% control more than 70%. The richest Americans own a greater proportion of the country's wealth than any time since the Crash of 1929. Despite the financial meltdown and subsequent bank bailout, Wall Street and the big corporations are recovering nicely, and, according to recent news reports, it's party time again for the rich, with hefty capital gains, big bonuses and outsized executive salaries.

To make matters worse, the next Republican Congress is on a path to enshrine many of the handouts and tax breaks that are little more than government welfare for the rich. All this as wealthy, anonymous donors flood Tea Party candidates with millions of dollars to safeguard the interests of the wealthy, all under the smokescreen of a "populist," anti-government agenda. Clearly, the average American has lost this latest battle for fairness and equality. But will we end up losing the war? Will the top one percent continue to consolidate their power and influence, essentially running the country from behind the smoke and mirrors of Republican legislation and conservative legal doctrine?

Americans as a people are generally slow to anger and usually reluctant to change. But once they get the message, they can be a pretty tough and determined group. For years before the Great Depression, Americans ignored the excesses of Wall Street and the bankers until economic calamity stared them in the face, at which point they stood up behind FDR as he remade the economy. As wars brewed in Europe, Americans sat on the sidelines until it became clear that they had to act, and then they did, strongly and decisively.

While we may be patient and slow to act, there will come a time when Americans wake up to the threat that is posed by the huge inequality in wealth that casts a shadow over the American dream. We may chuckle at the hapless auto executives who fly their private jets to testify before Congress, or grumble about the corporations that put profits before progress, hewing to the quarterly balance sheet rather than the real bottom line. We may patiently endure the environmental destruction by energy companies or the corrupt health insurance system, but eventually, we will wake up to the real harm that has been done to us all.

The current wave of populism is focused on the excesses of government, from Washington to the state capitals and the city halls of America. Certainly, there is a great waste of resources and human energy in all of our governments, which can also manifest itself in intrusion into our daily lives. But the excesses of government pale in comparison to the destructive effect of the extreme concentration of wealth and power in our society.

The plain fact is that all government -- federal, state and local -- is more beholden to the wealthy and powerful interests than any time in recent history. The influence of money in politics from wealthy individuals, multinational corporations and powerful lobbyists is enormous, and impacts every aspect of our lives. The problem is that their power is largely hidden, especially when compared to that of governments, which have become increasingly transparent in the last quarter of a century. The irony is that the Tea Partiers can attack government because it is largely open and responsive, while it is more difficult to attack the wealthy and powerful interests in our society, which operate largely out of the public eye.

The answer is not to punish those at the top, although we might look with envy at other countries who mete out severe punishment to corporate criminals as a way to signal that the theft of billions of dollars and the horrendous damage to our economy and nation are in fact serious crimes. Instead of parceling out justice to the wealthy who have benefited from inequality and injustice, we should strive instead to return to the ideals of the American dream, in which freedom, equality and justice are not just empty slogans on bumper stickers, but are guiding principles for all our citizens -- rich and poor, powerful and weak. If the American dream is restored as the common goal of our nation, then we may lose a few battles, but we will win the war.

Rooting for the Tea Party

September 2010

I am certainly no fan of the Tea Party -- they represent a dangerous and extremist facet of the American character. What's more, I disagree with the view that the Tea Party victories in the Republican primaries will provide a big electoral boost to the Democrats in the midterms. But there are a couple of ways in which the Tea Party could help the progressive cause. One is tactical, the other substantive.

First, the tactics. There are several dozen Republican-held Congressional seats in districts where Republicans hold less than a ten percent registration advantage over Democrats. In those districts, Tea Party candidates (not those who won Republican primaries) are flocking to run as independents. If history is any precedent, these candidates may be able to peel away as much as twenty percent of conservative Republican and Independent votes. This would put some Democratic challengers within striking distance of winning. For example, in the 26th District in California, entrenched Republican David Dreier has never faced serious competition in his nearly thirty years in office. (Full disclosure -- I was a candidate for this Congressional seat in 2006). The current Democratic nominee, Russ Warner, has only a modest war chest in comparison with Dreier's coffers, and limited name recognition. However, a Tea Party candidate, David Miller, has emerged as a conservative alternative to the entrenched Dreier. Miller's website reads like a Tea Party mantra, from its focus on the Constitution, free market principles and the Second Amendment to its opposition to health care reform and same-sex marriage.

In a district where registration of independents has boomed and voting for independent candidates doubled between 2004 and 2008, Miller may be able to capture a significant number of votes. All politics are local, and it is hard to predict how a disaffected electorate will vote on the local level, but a Tea Party challenger who attracts support from conservatives may pull enough votes away from incumbent Republicans to win back a few seats, even in a year when Democratic turnout could be low. In a midterm election year, a few seats could be enough to keep the House in Democratic hands.

Okay, so much for the tactics. What about the substantive boost that the Tea Party can provide progressives? Let's go back to the 2008 election, which was all about hope and change. Obama rode the crest of that wave, and then faced the harshest economic recession in nearly eighty years. Despite the incessant attacks and stonewalling by Republicans, President Obama still has higher midterm approval ratings than either Ronald Reagan or Bill Clinton. Perhaps more surprising -- given the constant drumbeat from Fox news and conservative talk show hosts -- is that voters have a more favorable view of Democrats than Republicans, even though they don't like either party very much.

So where does the Tea Party fit in? In my opinion, the Tea Partiers are simply the most extreme and reactionary expression of a much broader and deeper sentiment -- the desire for real political change. While the Tea Partiers snatch the headlines with their anti-government, xenophobic and even racist rants, most of the country is still committed to the kind of positive change that Obama promised during his "Yes, we can" campaign. The election of 2010 is not that much different. Most Americans still want constructive change in the country -- except that with the onset of the economic crisis, positive change is even more critical to our future.

And, speaking of our future, people also want hope. That is what has been missing from the Obama presidency up to this point. Instead of a message of hope, we have been getting policy discussions. Instead of inspiration, we've been getting a lesson in Washington sausage making. So far, Obama has failed to passionately pursue the cause of change and the message of hope, which the majority of Americans are still seeking. The 2008 election was not about a change of administration, or even a change in legislative priorities. It was about a change in the political culture. It was about listening carefully to the voice of the people - not the talking heads or the corporate interests or the party leaders -- and fighting for their cause.

FDR is still a great example of a leader who championed the message of hope and change. Sure, he told the American people it would be tough, but then he launched a massive effort for fundamental reform, despite blistering attacks from his opponents. And he was a vicious counterpuncher, knocking his enemies back on their heels when they opposed him. All the while, he repeated the message of hope, over and over again, promising the American people that together they would overcome adversity. The result was a great transformation of American society and politics that paved the way for the successes of the twentieth century. And, along the way, FDR created a powerful political coalition that would endure for more than sixty years. Remember, it wasn't the Tea Party that first brought up the idea of change in the political culture of this country. For many years, it has been the progressive movement that has championed advances in every level of American society -- from Social Security and Medicare to civil rights, equality of opportunity and freedom of choice. 2008 was a watershed election, an outcry from a large majority of Americans (not a tiny bunch of Tea Party extremists) for a fundamental change in the politics of our country. What the Tea Party movement reminds us is that the promise of change must not be abandoned to a few fanatics on the right who would march us backwards into a darker and less compassionate past.

Surviving A Republican Congress

September 2010

Political forecasters Charlie Cook and Stu Rothenberg both recently predicted that the Republicans are likely to win forty or more House seats in the midterm elections. While two months is an eternity in politics, it is worth considering what Republican control of the House would mean.

First and foremost, it will mean that Republicans will finally have to take some responsibility for governing the country. The 1994 Republican takeover emboldened Newt Gingrich and the conservative crowd to throw their weight around with the Contract with America, followed by the ill-advised decision to shut down, albeit temporarily, the entire federal government. As a result, President Clinton's approval ratings shot up as the Republicans' ratings tanked.

We can fully expect the Republicans to continue their stonewalling and obstructionism -- and probably even ramp it up with the addition of newer Republican House members drinking the Tea Party Kool-Aid. If they take over the House, they will not only be able to block President Obama's initiatives, but also launch their own agenda, which will undoubtedly include everything from repealing health care reform to gutting social programs. However, if the Republicans use their veto in the House to try to turn back the clock by eviscerating Medicare or Social Security, cutting unemployment or veterans benefits, or stripping funds from education or the state budgets, they could certainly face a wrathful public.

What would all this mean for the Obama White House? This administration came into office facing the worst economic downturn in eighty years, and, as a result, a sizeable chunk of the public has turned against Obama and the Democratic party. However, the public has certainly not morphed into big fans of the Republican party either. The populist sentiment now sweeping the nation -- as in times past -- is aimed at both parties and their leaders. The outcry from both the left and right is for a change in the political culture, which is besotted with money from special interests, relies on rigged electoral districts and is myopic about social changes in the country.

The reality is that, even with the populist hue and cry, around ninety percent of House incumbents will be re-elected (down from the usual 95% or more) and it will be back to business as usual, which means a virtual stalemate. If the House is controlled by the Republicans, an even more serious deadlock will ensue as

Republicans continue to stonewall the White House. If the economic recovery stalls out, this will put Obama in an even tougher position than FDR was in the midst of the Depression, when the Democrats had large majorities in the House and Senate.

What the president can do -- as FDR did when he encountered resistance both inside and outside his own party -- is to go over the head of the politicians to the American public. Although Obama has made lots of speeches and appeared frequently in public, the message has often been muted or confused. Like FDR, Obama would benefit by aggressively attacking his opponents on their policies -- whether it is cutbacks in Social Security or Medicare or extremist proposals like repealing the Fourteenth Amendment.

The Republican party, which is now driven by the radical viewpoints of Glenn Beck and Sarah Palin, should be vehemently called out by the president on their specific proposals to turn back the clock to a more intolerant and crueler America that persecuted minorities, demonized religious groups and left the old and disabled to suffer on their own. A more aggressive and focused message from the president is not only a good campaign strategy for the midterms but also is a stronger approach to governing, whether the Republicans take over the House or not.

Where is the "New Deal?"

September 2010

When Franklin Roosevelt accepted the Democratic nomination in 1932, he called for a "new deal" for the American people. He said that "throughout the nation, men and women" had been "forgotten" by their government. He added that this "new deal" would be more than a political campaign, it would be "a call to arms." Most Americans now think of the New Deal as a set of government programs, from Social Security to the Works Progress Administration. But, at its heart, the New Deal was renewal of the government's social contract with its citizens. FDR's convention speech was an acknowledgment that the government had failed the American people through mismanagement of the economy, lax oversight of the banks and its failure to look out for the welfare of a large majority of its citizens.

While Roosevelt's New Deal programs were violently attacked by both Republicans and Democrats as unconstitutional, socialist and un-American, and many were either scrapped or repealed, his pledge to form a new social contract between the government and the American people gained him the trust of a broad swath of working Americans. Although some historians have argued that FDR's programs were often ineffective in combating the scourges of the Great Depression, there is little dispute that Roosevelt forged a bond with the nation - the New Deal Coalition -- that endured for most of the twentieth century.

As economists and elected officials argue over the most effective tools for ending the Great Recession -- whether it be stimulus packages, tax cuts or austerity programs - the larger message of this crisis is being overlooked. Whether on the right or the left, from Tea Party activists to populist Democrats, the clear message from the American public is that the government is out of touch with the people. Or, to put it in grander terms, the social contract between the government and the governed is seriously strained.

The success of the Obama campaign in reaching out to independent voters -- who are the bellwether citizens in this era of political partisanship -- was largely due to his message of change. While the message was criticized for being overly vague, it clearly struck a chord with voters who understood that the government -- and more specifically the political class -- had become isolated and resistant to the kind of change that is essential to a democracy. As the Obama campaign correctly recognized, this was not an issue of left or right, but a more fundamental question of listening to the voice of the people.

There can be little debate that American political culture has become corrupted over the past thirty or so years. Money -- always the mother's milk of politics -- has now become virtually the entire diet of political life. The partisan ideological battles that seem to bitterly divide us are simply convenient tools for the political class to stir up emotions and distract the general public from the deep problems that are staring us in the face.

With the advent of the Great Recession, several facts have become abundantly clear. As a nation, we have been forced to re-examine our expectations for ourselves, our communities and ultimately our government. It is clear that the federal government -- and many state and local governments -- are too large and inefficient to accomplish the more modest goals that we must set for them. At the same time, the fundamental American principle of equality of opportunity has been assaulted by a concerted effort of the federal government and multinational corporations. The clearest evidence of this assault -- in 1970, the wealthiest 1% of Americans took home 9% of the nation's income; by 2007, the top 1% took home nearly 24% of total income.

While the strategies for recovery -- stimulus, austerity or tax cuts -- may be different on the right or on the left, the renewal of the social contract should be paramount, and is not that much different on either end of the political spectrum. Conservatives are correct that the political culture has become corrupt, and that government is often wasteful and ineffective. At the same time, progressives are right that America should not abandon its fundamental principle of equality of opportunity. When 1% of the citizens grab nearly one-quarter of the nation's income, the system is clearly rigged and needs to be reformed.

As in FDR's day, whatever programs President Obama proposes to address the tears in the political fabric will be bitterly attacked, probably from both sides of the aisle. However, the clear message from voters in the last election and ever since -- left, right and center -- was "Fix the political culture!" If the president embraces this more important, overriding message that voters are sending, he will be on the right track. And that means aggressively attacking opponents of change, no matter what party they belong to.

Remember that FDR famously attacked everyone who stood in the way of reform, no matter who they were. He unleashed a rhetorical firestorm against bankers (calling them "unscrupulous money changers" and "rulers of mankind's exchange of goods") and political opponents ("not content with attacking me, or my wife, or my sons, they now include my little dog Fala") While many Americans may have questioned the effectiveness of FDR's New Deal programs, they rarely questioned his dedication to them -- and his hope for a "new deal" between the government and the American people. As we struggle to recover from the depths of the Great Recession, Americans are again looking again for a "new deal" with their government.

A New Path to the Two-State Solution

September 2010

For more than seventy years, the "two-state solution" has been a negotiating point between Israel and the Palestinians. In negotiation after negotiation, the goal has been continuously restated, and yet seems ever more remote. With a right-wing coalition in power in Israel and a split between Fatah and Hamas in Palestine, and with both Israeli and Palestinian public opinion deeply pessimistic about any significant peace agreement arising from the talks that begin this week, the likelihood of a real two-state solution seems slim.

However, there are some hopeful signs, as pointed out in a recent *New York Times* article by Ethan Bronner, reporting from the Palestinian Authority city of Ramallah on the West Bank. In the piece, Bronner describes "increasingly reliable security forces, a more disciplined government and a growing sense among ordinary citizens that they can count on basic services." He cites economic growth in the West Bank as being up eleven percent over a year ago.

My own recent visit to Israel and the West Bank bears out much of what Bronner describes. Despite a heavy Israeli troop footprint, the presence of dozens of Jewish settlements and continuing hardship for ordinary Palestinians, there is a renewed vitality to life in Ramallah and the West Bank. For my Palestinian driver, who had expressed extreme skepticism about a negotiated solution -- along with most others, both Palestinians and Israelis, with whom I spoke -- the only moment of optimism and pride was when he drove me through Ramallah, pointing to Palestinian banks, hotels and upscale shops. As a veteran of many wars and the recent intifadas, the upsurge in economic growth on the West Bank was the sole glimmer of hope that I could see in his eyes.

As reported by Bronner and other observers, the push for economic growth, as well as the improvement in security, education and infrastructure, comes largely through the efforts of the Palestinian Prime Minister, Salam Fayyad. Fayyad represents a new approach to the two-state solution. Unlike the rejectionist tack taken by Hamas, or the diplomatic approach of Chairman Mahmoud Abbas, this avenue favors building the Palestinian state from the ground up, rather than top down through international agreements.

The theory is that if the Palestinian Authority can succeed economically, with improved security and infrastructure for its citizens, then it will be able to build *de facto* statehood without having to depend on fragile diplomatic accords. It will then be in a much stronger position to negotiate the thorny issues that remain, including its borders with Israel, Jewish settlements on the West Bank and the status of refugees. Success for the PA, of course, depends on international support both from the West and from Arab countries. So far, some support has been forthcoming, although there is still much progress to be made in terms of private investment.

Of course, this is the Middle East, where optimism for peace is in precious short supply. Both Chairman Abbas and Prime Minister Netanyahu of Israel are taking great risks by returning to the bargaining table. There will certainly be rejectionists on both sides who will fight -- both literally and metaphorically -- against the two-state solution. But, in the end, economic progress on the West Bank may undercut those who advocate violence and confrontation, as more and more Palestinians and Israelis see a sliver of hope for the future.

The Self-Destruction of the Republican Party

May 2010

The old joke about the Democratic party was that their political strategy was to circle the wagons and fire inward. Now the joke is on the Republicans, who seem determined to self-destruct, despite the most promising political climate for them since 1994. The comments last week by Republican Senate nominee Rand Paul illustrate the depth of this self-destruction. In one breathtaking ideological swoop, Mr. Paul questioned the soundness of the Civil Rights Act of 1964, as well as the Obama administration's criticism of British Petroleum in the midst of the largest oil spill in history.

Thirty years after the election of Ronald Reagan, how did the Republican party end up in this conservative cul-de-sac, conducting an ideological purge worthy of Robespierre? After all, this is a party with a long history of political moderates who have had an important impact on our nation, both as the loyal opposition and as leaders of the struggle for progress. Consider Republican Senator Edwin Brooke, the first African-American senator from Massachusetts, Republican Mark Hatfield, who co-sponsored a bill with George McGovern calling for the complete withdrawal of troops from Vietnam or Republican Howard Baker, who was a tough critic and investigator of President Nixon during Watergate?

Even Republican presidents Eisenhower, Nixon, Ford, Reagan and Bush, Sr. famously compromised on a host of issues, from criticizing the "military-industrial complex" and visiting Communist China to supporting national health care plans and raising taxes. Who dreamed that as Democrats we would someday pine for moderate Republicans in the mold of Nelson Rockefeller?

From a purely political standpoint, the Tea Party extremists are a godsend for Democratic politicians, since they offer up candidates like Rand Paul, who are the poster children for regressive, even racist, political ideologies. The specter of dismantling government programs at the level that Paul and his cohorts apparently contemplate is beyond frightening to most voters, who have come to regard programs like Social Security and Medicare as socially beneficial rather than as the evil fruits of socialist conspiracies.

The conventional wisdom has been that the Republican party will sweep back into power as the political pendulum shifts back to the party out of office. But the political world may be changing substantially. While Democrats in Congress are unpopular, President Obama has maintained much of the good will of the American people, especially in light of Republican stonewalling and the Tea Party lurch to the right. As the recent special congressional election in Pennsylvania demonstrates, even voters in a district that John McCain carried in 2008 are not persuaded to vote Republican simply on the basis of attacks on the Obama White House and the Reid-Pelosi Congress.

What the cowardly Republican leadership forgets is the political maxim that elections are generally decided between the lesser of two evils. By simply attacking President Obama and the Democrats while they ignore the outrageous and irresponsible elements within their own ranks, they are presenting themselves to voters as the more dangerous and destructive option in November. By condoning the most loud and extreme voices in their party, the Republican party is sowing the seeds of its own destruction.

Moral Blindness on Wall Street

April 2010

One of the most shocking elements of the testimony by Goldman Sachs executives this week was the moral blindness they showed when evaluating the economic collapse and the role of their firm in that catastrophe. Over and over again, the Goldman executives excused their role in the greatest downturn since the Great Depression as simply "market makers," as if that would exempt them from the most basic moral standards.

Since they were nothing but "market makers," argue the executives, they should not be held responsible for the most egregious kinds of conflict of interest, in this case aggressively selling of billions of dollars of synthetic collateralized debt obligations without disclosing to the buyers, the rating agencies or the regulators not only that they were "shorting" these products, but they had actually worked with a hedge fund to dump the most risky securities into the swaps.

What passes for morality on Wall Street is certainly as strange as the synthetic CDO's themselves. After all, who died and made Goldman and the other investment banks the singular gods of the American financial system? Clearly, the idea that we could ever trust Wall Street to be the sole, unregulated market makers of American finance is ridiculous, even though eight years of Republican rule apparently convinced these tarnished titans that they could rule without the slightest moral compass.

The fact that Goldman and the other investment banks ruled the financial roost does not justify their blatant conflicts of interest, unbridled greed and manipulation of the risk markets. The Senate hearings may have demonstrated not only that products like synthetic CDOs are complicated beyond comprehension, but that they represent a complete divorce of Wall Street from both common sense and simple morality.

As much as the bankers deny it, the financial system has been hijacked by traders, with most of their profits derived from speculating on exotic securities rather than any real banking or customer business. And this has been done with the nearly explicit permission of the government, which has been complicit in the moral blindness, and now is desperately attempting to corral the horse that has long since left the barn.

What is not complicated at all is the need for the Congress and the administration -- not to mention the American people -- to confront the moral blindness on Wall Street and quickly rein it in. Wall Street cannot be trusted to "make markets" with no oversight from a referee in the form of the federal government. For those who gripe that government regulation will inhibit free markets, the strong response is that is exactly what the government should be doing, especially when unfettered financial markets lead to the kind of spectacular meltdown that Wall Street has visited upon the global economy.

Is This Any Way to Run a Pop Stand?

April 2010

Imagine an organization that is hopelessly split into two warring factions. Neither side speaks to the other, and each continually blocks the other from taking any action. Instead of moving forward with a common agenda, the two sides spend most of their time personally vilifying each other, and squander most of the resources of the organization trying to defeat their opponents' plans. What if this organization was the biggest and most powerful in the world, determining the fate of hundreds of millions of people and responsible for trillions of dollars?

You guessed it -- this organizational nightmare is not a figment of some demented management consultant's brain -- it is none other than the United States Congress. Is it any wonder that they never get anything done? What business, school, church or non-profit could operate with this kind of organizational culture? Who would want to work in a place where open hostility among employees was not only tolerated, but encouraged? And who would fight tooth and nail for a job at an organization that is almost universally despised by the very people it is supposed to serve?

Winston Churchill famously remarked that "Democracy is the worst form of government except all those other forms that have been tried from time to time." Certainly, dysfunctional legislatures are practically a hallmark of democracy, and our Congress is no exception. It has never been a poster child for either efficiency or civility, but in the past decade, Congress has sunk to historic lows. What has gone wrong?

In a recent panel discussion at a conference of business economists, the political pollster and consultant Charlie Cook blamed the lack of personal interaction between the members of Congress for its current partisanship and incivility, not to mention its inability to address the most serious issues facing the nation. In an opinion piece explaining his decision to leave the Senate, Senator Evan Bayh wrote that there were only two occasions where he met with all of his Senate colleagues at other than purely ceremonial events -- once was after the 9/11 attacks. "There were no Republicans or Democrats in the room that day, just Americans," writes Bayh. "The spirit of patriotism and togetherness was palpable. That atmosphere prevailed for only two or three weeks before politics once again intervened. "

Cook and others have traced the rise in partisanship and the lack of social contact between members of Congress to the decision by Speaker Gingrich in 1994 to shorten the weekly sessions in the House and thus encourage members not to move their families to Washington. Gingrich's stated goal was to demonstrate a greater dedication to the political grassroots and prevent members from being overly swayed by the political culture of the capital. While the goal may have been admirable, the results have been disastrous. Coupled with the partisan redistricting of the past fifteen years, it has led to a dangerous disconnect from the common goal of public service. Even worse, it has made it much easier to demonize those on the opposite side of the aisle. Of course, there are lots of reasons for the vicious partisanship in Washington that have nothing to do with the lack of personal interaction across the aisle -- including the Tea Partiers and Fox's right-wing ideologues like Glen Beck, Sean Hannity and Bill O'Reilly, not to mention Sarah Palin. But a little more personal contact between members of Congress sure couldn't hurt.

As a child growing up in Washington in the 1960's -- my father worked in the Library of Congress and later in the State Department -- there was no partisanship on the Little League field, in PTA meetings or in church groups. My Cub Scout troop included the son of uber-liberal Hubert Humphrey, while the son of the former Republican Secretary of State was in my class at school. I wasn't old enough to understand how this might impact their work in Congress or at the White House, but I am sure that both Republican and Democratic parents talked about their kids' Little League games, or teachers at school. Once you have faced off at your children's soccer games or chatted at a church picnic, it is hard to treat your political opponents as faceless demons -- especially if you know that you are going to see them on the ballfield that weekend.

There are lots of fancy management techniques for team building that are justly ridiculed as so much wasted frou-frou. Certainly, no one would suggest "trust exercises" for Nancy Pelosi or John Boehner. But Congress could certainly use a timeout from the relentless partisan sniping, something like the World War I Christmas truce when German and Allied soldiers came out of the trenches to sing a couple of songs together. For starters, how about a little bit of casual, off-the-record socializing? Maybe a Friday afternoon -- bring the spouse and kids along for some ice cream and pizza? Only one rule -- no politics allowed.

Democrats, White Men and the Tea Party Revolt

March 2010

In his fine book *The Neglected Voter: White Men and the Democratic Dilemma*, David Paul Kuhn took a hard look at the future of the Democratic party, and it's not good news. Since 1972, white men have voted by well over 60% for Republican or conservative candidates in every single presidential race. The only exceptions were Jimmy Carter, who got 48% of the white male vote, and Barack Obama, who got 41% of white men.

What does this say about the future of the Democratic party and progressives, especially with the rise of the vocal -- though small and disorganized -- Tea Party movement? With the minority and youth vote expected to be significantly lower in the 2010 midterm elections, white voters will likely cast more than 75% of the ballots. And with Obama's approval ratings in the mid-30's among white men, the Democrats' hold on Congress is in jeopardy and Obama's re-election in 2012 is questionable.

While some argue that the more progressive blocs of minorities and women voters can overcome the conservative votes of white men, Kuhn points out the fallacy of that argument. The nearly 100 million white men make up almost 40% of the American electorate, more than five times the total of all Hispanic voters, male and female. And the slight improvement that Democrats have registered with white women voters (over half of whom still vote regularly for Republicans) doesn't begin to match the Republican party's enormous advantage among white men. Add to that the outsized influence of the white male vote in the South (where more than 75% of white men vote Republican) and in rural areas which carry heavy weight in the electoral college (one Wyoming resident's vote equals the vote of seventy-two Californians), the electoral future for progressives looks dim.

In the short term, these dismal demographics argue for an aggressive legislative agenda for the Democrats while they hold the majority in Congress and while President Obama remains personally popular (although the coming months will reveal whether his popularity can be sustained in the wake of the health care bill). Certainly, a focus on jobs is paramount, since men have been the major losers in the current employment landscape. However, even if the White House has a hyper-focus on jobs in the next few months, unless the jobs outlook improves, the midterm elections look bleak for Democrats.

In the longer term, Democrats need to face the gender gap squarely. This does not mean capitulating on progressive causes, nor does it mean competing with Republicans on the macho quotient or reshaping itself as the "daddy" party. What the Democrats - and progressives in general - need to do is revive their conversation with white men, much as they did with African-Americans in the 1950's and with women in the 1960's and '70's. Rather than seeing the world in terms of gender, race, ethnicity or other specific interest, Democrats need to see the world in broader, 21st century terms.

There can be no disputing that white men - like all Americans - are suffering in the most severe economic downturn since the Depression. Men who were able to support their families with good jobs have been thrown onto the street - in some cases literally - through no fault of their own. For the traditional male - and all men have at least some traditional male in them - this is a severe blow to their self-esteem. And while our society has justly recognized the injustices done to women, minorities and other groups in our society, we have been slow to recognize injustices done to white men, who have been viewed as occupying a privileged place in society (even though the vast majority of white men enjoy no such privileges).

As we strive for a post-racial society, where citizens enjoy equal rights and privileges despite their race or national origin, our goal as progressives should be a for post-gender society, where men and women of all races are treated with dignity and respect. And perhaps more importantly, our goal should be a society in which all groups - including white men - are included in the conversation about our future. This is not a simple task, since modern psychology - and our own common sense - tells us that men and women have very different ways of not only conversing, but of relating to the world. Just as Democrats have urged their leaders, beginning with Bill Clinton, to "feel the pain" of the voters as a way to relate to women, so Democrats now should learn how to connect with the emotions of white male voters.

The Tea Party movement seeks to return us to a divisive past by capitalizing on the anger - largely of white men - against the injustices and neglect that they feel. In this way, the Tea Partiers most resemble, in their tactics if not in substance, the leftist movements of the 1930's, which used economic distress to fuel a rebellion against the capitalist system. To his great credit, FDR opened a dialogue with disenfranchised workers, who had been largely neglected and even scorned by much of American society. Even though FDR rarely compromised his policy positions (he was anything but a socialist), he managed to gain the confidence of a large swath of the American work force, and kept them from falling under the spell of political extremism.

FDR not only saved America from extremism, but he also a built a powerful, progressive political movement that was a voice for all disenfranchised Americans - from workers to minorities to women. Democrats have a chance to rebuild that progressive movement, but only if they listen to another disaffected group - white men. This does not mean that progressives must abandon the causes and the groups that they have championed for decades. But it does mean that we should listen carefully to the concerns of white men - urban and rural, North and South - and respond to them within the framework of progressive values. Only then will we be able build a more inclusive future for our country -- one that does not include the divisive hatred and venom of the Tea Partiers.

Bridging the Partisan Divide Through "Intentional Conversation"

March 2010

In the late 1990's, the country music industry was in a slump. Revenues, which had quadrupled over the previous decade, were anemic. Vicious competition between the record companies was rife, poisoning the atmosphere throughout the industry and dampening the enthusiasm of music fans. During this period, a colleague of mine was asked to organize a weekend meeting of country music executives to address the problems of the industry. These executives were bitter enemies, many of whom had not spoken in years, except for the public broadsides launched across a bitter divide.

After the initial challenge of getting everyone in a room together, my colleague faced the enormous obstacle of engaging the executives in some form of civil discourse. Rather than announcing an agenda or going right to the contentious issues plaguing the industry, he decided to dispense with an agenda and simply begin a conversation. He asked the executives to talk about themselves -- their backgrounds, their families and their interests outside of work. As the conversation became increasingly personal, the bitter animosity began to slowly melt and the executives exchanged stories about their lives.

What emerged was not an action agenda for their business, but rather a realization that virtually everyone in the room had a shared common interest -- their love of country music. Rather than bickering over industry standards or haggling over deal points, the executives were swapping memories of great performers they had known and the songs they loved. And rather than being divided by their own narrow self-interests, they were united in a higher, common purpose -- the future of country music. While this meeting may have played only a role, country music sales grew by more than twelve percent over the next decade, while overall music industry sales declined by twenty percent.

Today, America itself faces a similar dilemma. Our leaders are bitterly divided and are barely on speaking terms. While Democrats and Republicans meet weekly in their caucuses, they virtually never cross party lines for joint meetings, even to chat and socialize with their colleagues. Sen. Evan Bayh (D-Ind.) has written in *The New York Times* that there were only two occasions where he met with all of his Senate colleagues at other than purely ceremonial events. Once was after the 9/11 attacks. "There were no Republicans or Democrats in the room that day, just Americans," writes Bayh. "The spirit of patriotism and togetherness was palpable. That atmosphere prevailed for only two or three weeks before politics once again intervened. "

Imagine a company or an organization that is dedicated to a common goal and, at the same time, is divided into two warring groups who barely communicate with each other except in public diatribes? Not only would the organization accomplish very little, but it would not be a very pleasant place to work. It may not be possible to wave a magic wand to dissolve all the substantive differences between the parties -- as President Obama discovered in his recent televised health care summit. However, it is possible to restore some civil discourse to Congress -- and hopefully to the country -- by improving the quality of the conversation.

Michel de Montaigne, the sixteenth-century French essayist wrote: "The most fruitful and natural exercise of our mind is conversation." What he had in mind was not a conference or a committee meeting, but a fundamental exchange of thoughts and feelings between human beings, beyond the narrow concerns of their daily lives. For more than a decade, I have worked with civic, business and religious leaders to organize a series of day-long "Intentional Conversations" that focus on the genuine exchange of ideas and personal experiences rather than simply on debate or a set of policy goals. These Conversations have brought together people of different political perspectives, religious faiths, genders, races and ages for a few hours of focused conversation, away from the distractions of modern life, and have often had a profound impact on the lives of the participants.

While the Conversations are structured around a larger discussion theme, their most memorable aspects are the small, personal moments that the participants share. Men and women who barely know one another -- and often only on a professional basis -- end up sharing some of their most personal experiences, as well as their hopes and dreams. In the course of a few hours, the broad chasms of gender, race, age, religious faith -- and, yes, even political belief -- are bridged through the process of genuine conversation. While few minds are changed, most participants emerge from the day with a greater understanding and empathy for the differences that divide us. The eminent historian of religion, Martin Marty, has said: "Argument begins with an answer, but conversation begins with a question." Human beings are by nature curious -- and our curiosity about our fellow humans is a powerful engine for understanding and appreciating our differences. The leaders of our country can take the first step toward healing the great partisan divide by engaging in a real conversation with their colleagues.

Why not a few hours of genuine, "intentional" conversation each month for all members of Congress? These should not be media events, and they certainly shouldn't be expected to dissolve the partisan rancor quickly. But they might offer the faint beginnings of a more civil dialogue in our country, along with the hope that, like the leaders of the country music industry, our leaders will be guided by not by narrow political interests, but by their shared love of America.

A Path to Victory in 2010

January 2010

While the prospects for Democrats in the 2010 midterm elections are looking grim, there is a path to victory -- if we decide to take it. The populist tide that swept Scott Brown to victory in Massachusetts and propelled the tea party protests over the past year, is essentially the same wave of sentiment that Barack Obama rode to the White House. President Obama himself acknowledged that fact in an interview this week with ABC News:

The same thing that swept Scott Brown into office swept me into office. People are angry and they are frustrated - not just because of what's happened in the last year or two years, but what's happened over the last eight years.

So what has happened over the last eight years? To put it bluntly, the government has lost touch with the American people. First, it was the misguided war in Iraq and the corruption in Congress, then the mishandling of Katrina, the bank bailouts and, most recently, the protracted health care reform effort that has turned into a game of Washington insiders and industry lobbyists. Not to mention the drumbeat of constant bickering and partisanship between Democrats and Republicans.

Talk show pundits on the left and the right make this out to be a battle of ideologies, of philosophies of government or of policy. But they are simply wrong. This is a fight over representative government, plain and simple. The majority of the American people want leaders who represent them -- not on every single issue of policy or even of values -- but on the core issues that are most important to them. Most people don't give a fig about ideology, but when it comes to what is important to their families and communities, they will very quickly step up and fight.

Right now, what is most important to Americans is the dire state of our economy. And it's not about the economy in some abstract sense -- it's about your neighbor down the street who got laid off or your sister who was furloughed. It's about your own job, and whether or not it will exist in six months or a year. It's about making your mortgage payment or paying for day care for your child. These are the issues that have focused the minds of Americans on their government and spurred a populist revolt.

Americans are famous for their common sense, justifiably so. They understand that our economic woes run deep, and that the government does not have the power to instantly turn things around. However, what they do expect is that our leaders -- in the face of the worst economic crisis since the Great Depression -- will focus single-mindedly on doing whatever they can to create jobs and revitalize the economy. Our leaders have not done that, and now the citizen revolt is in full swing. Of course, health care reform is important, as are the wars in Iraq and Afghanistan, along with a host of other issues. But all that pales in comparison to the 800-pound gorilla of the economic crisis, which is way at the top of citizen concerns in all opinion polls. Whether they are Democrats, Republicans or independents, our leaders ignore these polls at their peril.

Both parties go into the 2010 elections with the headwind of a populist revolt. For the Democrats, they will face the wrath that voters naturally direct at the party in power. As for the Republicans, voters are disgusted by their stubborn refusal to address the economic crisis and their adopting the purely political tactic of stonewalling. "A pox on all your houses," is the voters' response. In the end, it doesn't really matter which party you come from. The path to victory in 2010 will be a vigilant focus on the economy. Whether the mantra is "jobs, jobs, jobs" or "it's the economy, stupid," politicians need to wake up and focus on what voters are saying, beyond the racket of Beltway punditry.

For Democrats, the good news is that Republicans are offering no viable alternative to revitalizing the economy. Voters recognize this and will respond to any candidate, regardless of party affiliation, who starts paying attention to what they want. President Obama has only lately gotten this message. But, frankly, this is not about Obama, who is not running again until 2012. This is about candidates for Congress -- both incumbents and challengers -- who have a rare opportunity to stand up for what has always been a cornerstone of Democratic principles.

The Democratic party has long been the champion of working, middle-class people and has a strong record of economic growth. From FDR and JFK to Lyndon Johnson and Bill Clinton, Democrats have been the party of growth and prosperity. It makes no sense that, during a time of grave economic crisis, the party should be distracted by social wedge issues or even important priorities like health care that do not address the fundamental economic problems faced by ordinary Americans.

If Democratic candidates in 2010 will return to solid representative politics on the local level -- listening to voters and addressing their concerns -- then they will stand a fighting chance, whether as incumbents or challengers, to withstand the populist firestorm. In fact, they may become better leaders in the process, and more truly representative of the people they seek to represent.

A Regional Summit on the War in Afghanistan

October 2009

As President Obama and his advisors debate a strategic change in the war in Afghanistan, it has become increasingly clear that this war has become a regional conflict that stretches into Pakistan, and even India and beyond. While the original rationale for the war was the elimination of a sanctuary for Al Qaeda, the conflict has now broadened into threats presented by a Taliban-controlled Afghanistan and, even more ominously, by a nuclear-armed and destabilized Pakistan.

While the recommendation by General Stanley McChrystal to bolster the counterinsurgency effort represents an advance in tactical military thinking, it ignores some of the fundamental political realities of the conflict. A lengthy and focused counterinsurgency effort might eventually produce results, but its chances of success are greatly diminished by the political climate in Afghanistan. Given the difficult choice between a Taliban that offers security and justice in countryside - albeit in the most harsh and backward forms - and a central government that is distant and corrupt, most Afghans outside of Kabul are forced to choose the Taliban. No foreign counterinsurgency effort can combat that kind of logic, especially when classic counterinsurgency tactics would call for more than 600,000 troops to do the job, a level that few Americans would support.

One of the early mistakes, among many, of the Bush administration in its invasion of Iraq was the failure to develop an international and regional consensus for action. The rationale was that most nations would not support the invasion, and it was a waste of time to focus on international cooperation. Thanks in large part to the insistence of Colin Powell, the Bush administration did take its case to the United Nations, where Powell presented trumped-up intelligence to sell the UN on the Bush plan. However, history has shown that no sincere effort was ever made to include our allies or the nations in the region in the decision to go to war.

As the years have gone by - Afghanistan is now the longest war in American history - it has become clear that the stakes are no longer the continued existence of Al Qaeda or even the stability of Afghanistan, but rather the dangers presented by a crumbling, nuclear-armed Pakistani state. To complicate matters further, the Pakistanis themselves have not - until very recently - perceived Afghanistan and the Taliban as a regional threat. In fact, elements of the Pakistani government, including the ISI intelligence service, have continued to provide strategic support to the Taliban insurgency.

Before the United States implements a unilateral change in military and political strategy in Afghanistan, wouldn't it be a good idea to seek regional cooperation for the strategy? This means not only Afghanistan and Pakistan, but also India, China and Russia. Certainly there are dangers in a regional summit, and it clearly should not be a public summit. But the idea that the United States can go it alone yet again without some kind of regional support is highly doubtful. Can't the Obama administration - with all its powerful persuasive tools - hold the feet of the regional players to the fire and mold a common strategy? Perhaps not, but without some consensus, the chances of failure in our longest war are even greater.

Does President Obama – or America – Deserve the Nobel Peace Prize?

October 2009

In the hours after the surprise announcement that President Obama had won the Nobel Peace Prize, the main argument seems to be whether the President -- and by extension America -- deserves the prize. After all, the argument goes, Obama has only been in office a few months, what has he done to deserve this prestigious prize that has been awarded to the likes of Nelson Mandela, Lech Walesa and Mother Theresa. And why give a prize, in effect, to America, when we have been responsible for two recent wars and the torture of terror suspects?

Alfred Nobel, the inventor of dynamite and a major armaments manufacturer, specified that the Peace Prize be given "to the person who shall have done the most or the best work for fraternity between nations, for the abolition or reduction of standing armies and for the holding and promotion of peace congresses." Although the Committee has strayed somewhat from its original mandate to honoring organizations rather than persons, including the Red Cross, the Friends Service Committee and Doctors Without Borders, the prizes to individuals have fallen into two general categories.

The first are those individuals who have struggled, often in obscurity and with few resources, to promote peace through advocacy for a specific issue or community. In the case of Mother Theresa, for the poor. Or for Mandela and Walensa, for the disenfranchised. The other category are world leaders -- from presidents and prime ministers to leaders of international organizations -- who have brought their power and influence to bear in the cause of peace - everyone from Theodore Roosevelt to Mohamed ElBaradei.

Beyond these categories, the underlying tone of the Nobel Committee's awards has been activist. While some of the awards are given simply for a person's past accomplishments, most of the prizes were awarded to individuals whose causes the committee wanted to spotlight or even promote. For example, in 1994, when the committee awarded the prize to Yasser Arafat, Yitzhak Rabin and Shimon Peres, it was not because of their lifetime dedication to the cause of peace. The prize was awarded in the hope that this gesture might help promote the Middle East peace effort. In a sense, then, the Nobel Peace Prize are awarded as much to people who are symbols of peace as to those who have devoted extensive efforts to the cause of peace.

But does President Obama -- and America -- deserve the peace prize? Near the end of his administration during a foreign trip, President Bush was asked by a foreign reporter whether America itself was not the greatest threat to world peace by dint of its unprovoked invasion of Iraq, its torture of terror suspects and its alienation of both its allies and unaligned nations with its bellicose rhetoric. Bush emphatically disagreed and called the question itself "absurd." However, many Americans and even more in the international community believed that this was, in fact, a fair question, and that the United States in the eight years of the Bush administration had embarked on a path that endangered world peace.

Through a combination of revulsion at the excesses of the Bush administration and the near collapse of the global economy, Americans voted in unprecedented numbers for Barack Obama. More than a repudiation of the Bush administration, Obama's election was seen as America turning a corner -- several corners, in fact. The first was the rejection of the Bush foreign and domestic policy, which had left the United States fighting two risky wars and with a crumbling economy. In addition, the election of Obama represented a new era in American politics and society -- the first African-American president. Both of these are powerfully symbolic milestones not only for Americans, but for the entire world.

Ever since Barack Obama stepped out of obscurity onto the platform of the Democratic National Convention in 2004 -- a powerful moment for all of us in the convention hall and around the world -- Americans have stepped forward to support this agent of change. The grassroots organization that turned out to work hard for Obama -- and give money in unprecedented amounts -- is testimony to both the symbolic power of hope and change. It is worth remembering that this movement to change America did not begin when Barack Obama took the presidential oath of office -- it has been underway for decades and has only now reached its culmination with the Obama presidency.

So my answer to the question is, yes, Obama and America do deserve the Nobel Peace Prize. The change that Obama has brought already to America has rippled out across the globe and restored the promise of peace and freedom that America represents. While those on the far left -- and far right -- who say that America doesn't deserve a Nobel Prize, I beg to differ. We can be proud of the hard-fought and hard-won change. My hope is that we can continue to fulfill the promise of America's new direction.

Civil Discourse and the "Intentional Conversation"

October 2009

The outbursts over the past month by Congressman Joe Wilson, Kanye West and Serena Williams have provoked much soul-searching in the media and the public in general about the level of civility in society. There are lots of theories about how rude and inconsiderate behavior has begun to permeate both our public and private discourse. Some blame celebrity culture, while others believe it a result of the partisan political culture. While there has been a lot of finger-pointing, there have been very few constructive suggestions about improving the level of the conversation beyond platitudes like "respecting our differences" or repeating the Golden Rule.

For nearly a decade, there has been a quiet though effective effort to improve the level of conversation, albeit in a modest community way. Since 1999, a series of Intentional Conversations has brought together civic, religious, business and cultural leaders for a day of genuine conversation. The Intentional Conversations (in which I have been an active participant), begun by the Skirball Institute on American Values and now sponsored by Marymount College in Palos Verdes, California, stress communication over confrontation and exchange of ideas over argument and sloganeering. The result has been what most participants describe as a unique and memorable opportunity for real conversation - a commodity that is sorely lacking in our fast-paced, competitive and confrontational world.

What is an Intentional Conversation? Stated simply: It is a structured conversation with no purpose other than the conversation itself. Or as Michel de Montaigne, the sixteenth-century French essayist wrote: "The most fruitful and natural exercise of our mind is conversation." Because of our hectic lives, the millions of distractions of modern life and the fallout from information overload, few of us have the time or discipline to devote ourselves to even a few hours of focused conversation. So the Intentional Conversation provides the structure - and the setting - to enjoy those few hours of conversation.

The other important element of an Intentional Conversation is that it has no stated purpose beyond the conversation itself. This is a critical component of the Intentional Conversation and what makes it different from any other gathering that comes with an agenda. We have all been to conferences which were devoted to a topic, or to solving a set of problems. While these serve a valuable purpose, they are not "conversations" in the same way as the Intentional Conversation, since their focus is on an agenda or a problem rather than on the conversation itself.

What also distinguishes the Intentional Conversations, both in theory and in practice, is the emphasis on the personal experiences of the participants. An

Intentional Conversation of 80-90 participants, for example, is broken down into small groups of 8-9 people. In the first of three hour-long small group sessions, the participants introduce themselves -- their backgrounds, their experiences and often talk about their beliefs and values. In these introductory conversations, I have been struck by how little we know about our fellow human beings from first impressions - the CEO whose ambition was to run a deli, the preacher who was influenced by his convict uncle or the woman from Russia who never knew her parents.

After the first session, there is often a panel discussion around the specific theme of the day. Past themes have included everything from "Living on the Edge of Eternity: Confronting Our Mortality" to "Personal Values and Political Beliefs: Exploring the Relationship Between Our Life Experiences and Political Identification" Following the panel, there is a second small group conversation in which participants relate their personal experiences to the theme of the Intentional Conversation. In the final small group conversation, participants link their personal experiences and values to the larger, more universal scope of the theme.

What I have found is that the reflections on the theme are less important than the personal experiences that the participants share in relation to the theme. Rather than coming up with a set of "bullet points" or resolutions, the participants emerge with a sense of having experienced a genuine exchange of views and feelings -- what one commentator has called the "essential conversation" which occurs as the participants focus on conversation for its own sake. These "essential conversations" often reach a depth or scope far beyond what might have occurred within the range of a narrow agenda. Because the only boundaries are the ground rules of the conversation structure, participants are able to pursue the conversational journey wherever it leads, which is often down profound and challenging pathways. The eminent historian of religion Martin Marty has said: "Argument begins with an answer, but conversation begins with a question." I would add that the Intentional Conversations generally end with even more questions than they begin with, which after all may be the point of conversation.

So what does the Intentional Conversation experience have to say about the lack of civility in our society? How can the lessons of the Intentional Conversation provide some answers to the argumentative and confrontational tone on the airwaves, in town hall meetings and even in our own living rooms? My favorite example is not from the Intentional Conversation, but from a real world case of how to restore civility and ultimately human cooperation. A colleague of mine is often called upon to lead high-level retreats for leaders in the entertainment industry - a volatile group in a volatile industry. A few years ago, he was asked to lead a retreat for leaders in the country music industry, which was undergoing severe challenges, in part because of the bitter rivalry between the major companies and players.

After a weekend of structured conversations, in which the bitter rivals shared some of their backgrounds and personal experiences, the participants were surprised to discover that while their daily lives were consumed by the fierce competition in the industry and the profit-and-loss statements of their companies, most of them shared a love of country music, which was what brought them into the business in the first place. Once they realized their common passion for music, they formed a bond which enabled them to see beyond their petty concerns and determine to work to for the good of an industry which the loved, and which was suffering.

Ultimately, the lessons of the Intentional Conversations are that when people share their personal experiences and values, they have a much greater understanding and tolerance for each other's opinions. With very few exceptions, when people of different backgrounds, political and religious beliefs and even value systems are able to converse with each other and truly connect, bridges of communication and understanding emerge. One stark example was the dispute between Harvard professor Henry Louis Gates and Cambridge police Sergeant Joseph Crowley that led to Gates' arrest. While there was much animosity at the time, a subsequent conversation, refereed by the President and Vice-President, evidently led to a genuine exchange and reconciliation.

While most of us don't have the benefit of participating in an Intentional Conversation or having the White House patch up our differences, we can draw a lesson from these events. The natural human curiosity that leads us to learn about our fellow human beings is the best guide when our passions threaten to get the better of us. If we think in terms of conversation rather than confrontation, exchange of ideas rather than argument, we will find our better angels there for guidance. Above all, if we see our fellow human beings for the complex and fascinating individuals they are rather than trying to mold them into caricatures, we will, without even thinking about it, elevate the level of civility all around us.

Crunch Time for the Democrats

October 2009

While the media has been filled with images of raucous town hall meetings and "tea party" protests from right wingers, these are largely irrelevant sideshows. The real pitched battle is within the Democratic party -- a battle that could determine the future of the Democrats as the governing party. In fact, the town hall circuses and the extremist rantings of right-wing talk radio have been a blessing in disguise for the Democrats, distracting the public from the growing intraparty schism in the halls of Congress.

But as the weather cools and the hard work of passing a health care bill begins this fall, the attention of the media and the public will turn away from right-wing ranters and directly onto the Democrats in Congress. Since virtually no Republicans will vote for health care legislation that is DOA in their districts, the question is whether enough Democrats in the House and Senate will vote to pass health care reform.

While the Blue Dog Democrats -- those who are most likely to lose their seats by voting for an unpopular health care bill -- are the first bloc of Democrats who have to be won over by the White House and the Democratic leaders, the liberal members of the House also have to be convinced to vote for whatever diluted version of health care reform emerges in the next few weeks. Although the House members from liberal districts don't have to worry about their jobs, they certainly have to be prepared to face the wrath of progressive voters who don't want to see the public option compromised.

On the most basic level, this gets down to old-fashioned political vote counting. Democratic members of Congress who face losing their jobs or displeasing most of the voters in their districts will think very carefully about voting for health care reform, even if it means a defeat for the President and their own party. However, if the Democrats in Congress fail to pass health care reform, they will be dealing both President Obama and, perhaps even more so, the Democratic party, a terrible blow.

Ironically, the President is in a better position to survive a defeat of health care reform than many Democrats in Congress. Unlike House Democrats, Obama has three years before he has to face the voters again. And he can certainly, and with justification, blame his own party for sending reform down in flames. While the President will of course aim to salvage health care reform, it will ultimately be up to the House Democrats to decide the fate of the bill.

If the Democratic party becomes irrevocably divided over health care reform, it will seriously threaten their majority in Congress, and call into question their ability to govern. Although it is unlikely that the public will embrace the Republican party, which is held captive by the extreme right wing, voters could well return to traditional voting patterns in 2010, particularly in swing districts, where they could throw out many freshman Blue Dogs, who account for the current strong House majority.

Since President Obama has arguably less to lose in this battle -- he could suffer a severe but not fatal setback -- it is the Democratic party itself, specifically the leadership in Congress, that needs to take a pivotal role in passing health care reform. Leaders of the liberal wing of the party -- not necessarily the elected leadership of the House -- must use their powers of persuasion and their skills in compromise to sway the debate in favor of change, most critically with progressive voters.

This is a moment of great opportunity to change the direction of health care policy in the United States. No solution will be perfect. Change will not come overnight. Some may deride this as "incremental change" when more fundamental reform is required. But even incremental change can be an important, positive beginning not only in improving our health care system, but in restoring responsible, responsive leadership to the governance of our nation.

The Gift of Ted Kennedy

August 2009

Ted Kennedy held a special place in the hearts of my family, my friends and my generation. My father, Roger Hilsman, worked for President Kennedy in the early '60s when Ted was "the kid brother" who came to the Senate at the tender age of 31, only to be welcomed with boatloads of skepticism about his qualifications for the office. Ted was the younger brother who marched behind John Kennedy's casket down Pennsylvania Avenue, trailing a riderless horse. He was the younger brother who delivered a stirring, halting eulogy for Robert Kennedy in Washington's National Cathedral.

Ted was also the man who took charge of the Kennedy family legacy, tirelessly and with great good humor. He assumed the leadership of the liberal wing of the Democratic party with an unmatched vigor and steadfastness through many discouraging years in the wilderness. But when he disagreed with his own party, he never failed to speak out, and even put his career on the line, as in 1980 when he challenged President Carter.

Despite his core commitment to liberal values and principles, he always managed to maintain strong friendships across party lines, even though he was often vilified by the right wing. In the Senate, he was universally admired as a fair opponent and strong leader, who was looking for solutions to problems, rather than seeking to simply pick a fight. He was also a terrific campaigner, as I witnessed first hand in several campaigns, including my own father's campaign for Congress in Connecticut in 1972, when Ted made a special point of speaking on my father's behalf to an enthusiastic audience of shipworkers in Norwich.

Ted Kennedy was a man who loved people, which is the very best quality a politician can have. Lots of politicians love "the people" in the abstract, but have very little use for people in real life. Ted was a man who clearly enjoyed interacting with everyone from conservative Senators to dockworkers or senior citizens. He also had another important quality for a politician - a clear set of values and beliefs that sprung from his own family, heritage and faith. No one could dispute the pedigree of his principles, and this gave him both great strength and a great burden.

Ted Kennedy's illness and death in the midst of a great national debate over health care is in every sense a terrible loss, not only of Ted as a beacon of strength in a epic battle, but also as a leader capable of reason and compromise. At the funeral of his brother Robert in 1968, Ted expressed the hope that, "What he was for us and what he wished for others will someday come to pass for all the world."

Perhaps his death will inspire us to follow our better angels and return to finding real solutions to the crisis in health care, rather than descending into shouting and slogans. This could be the final gift of Ted Kennedy.

The Modesty of Hope

August 2009

The debate over health care reform has rapidly morphed from a discussion of the risks and rewards of proposals to improve our health care system into a much larger, broader debate that has very little to do with health care. In town hall meetings and on cable networks, in blogs and over dinner tables, we are now arguing about our hopes and expectations for the American Dream.

Since the dawn of the Industrial Age, and even before, there has been a deep strain of exceptionalism in the American character. The idea is that America and Americans are somehow special, masters of our own destiny in a chaotic and uncertain world, able to exert both our moral leadership and economic might to lift humanity to a higher place. With the misguided war in Iraq and the economic missteps that lead to the greatest economic meltdown since the Depression, American exceptionalism -- and with it the American Dream -- has been brought sharply into question.

Even President Obama's "audacity of hope" rings with echoes of American exceptionalism. "We are a great people" was the implication, "and if we simply recommit ourselves to the American Dream, we can again triumph over adversity and despair." After a rough month in which the health care debate escalated into a screaming match and Americans began again to view the national glass as half-empty, questions about exceptionalism and the American Dream have resurfaced.

The health care debate has become a microcosm for those questions. Essentially, there are three critical issues at play in the health care discussion -- equity, efficiency and quality of care. The health care system is clearly inequitable -- only those who can afford insurance or who have no pre-existing conditions will be given full access to medical care. The system is also clearly inefficient -- we spend more on health care than most nations and have poorer results. And the quality of care is uneven -- it ranges from unrivaled Cadillac treatment for some conditions and individuals to extreme neglect in areas like preventive care and care for the uninsured.

Each of these critical issues has its advocates on both sides of the political spectrum. While some want more equity in the system, others would like to see more efficiency, and still others fear a loss of quality care. But what few of the proponents of the various policy positions acknowledge is that there are not many realistic, affordable options that address these issues. Universal, single payer coverage is likely beyond our means, certainly at the level of care we now provide. The European nations and Japan have discovered this and are facing their own health care crises. Efficiency in the health care system is unlikely to come quickly and will certainly not provide the cost savings that many people -- including the President -- envision. And, finally, the high quality health care that has been delivered in the past, albeit inequitably and inefficiently, is no longer affordable.

What this means is that we, as Americans, must accept at some level, an unequal, inefficient, lower-quality health care system. Right now, most people are not willing to do that. They want to cling to what they have, even if it means an expensive, cumbersome system. In the end, it is the devil we know rather than the devil we don't know. However, America's corporations and businesses have announced with great clarity that they are no longer willing to pick up the tab for an expensive and inefficient system. At that point, the only other payer is the American government, i.e. taxpayer, who will pay either in the form of subsidies or a direct government program.

We are, therefore, at one of those peculiar moments in history when our destiny is clear, but we are unwilling to embrace it fully. The American Dream has been diminished, and we can no longer rely on American exceptionalism -- or even the audacity of hope -- to restore it. What we can do, however, with modesty and humility, is to accept our somewhat diminished circumstances and, counting our many blessings, proceed to forge a path forward that preserves our fundamental American values of equality, integrity and common sense. Perhaps it is audacious to hope -- as President Obama did in his campaign -- that we can come together to forge a common solution to adversity. But we must begin with modest hopes and modest goals.

The New Voice in Health Care Reform: Voters

August 2009

One of the first lessons that any politician should learn is to listen -- really listen -- to the voters. This is not as easy as it sounds, because voters are not like policy wonks. They don't list the pros and cons of specific pieces of legislation or weigh the fiscal impact of a bill. They are too busy going to work and raising their families. Only when voters get really riled up do they send their message -- loud and clear -- to public officials. Hence the growing public debate over reform.

The debate over health care reform is one of those instances where politicians need to listen very carefully to what voters are saying, and what the voters really want. What's more, politicians and public officials need to take a much closer look at the political realities of health care in America. While there was a lot of discussion about health care during the presidential campaign and in its aftermath, most of the public had only a very foggy notion of what health care reform would mean to them. Only now are they forming more cogent opinions, and this fact alone could present a grave threat to health care reform efforts.

To begin with, "health care reform" is, in purely political terms, an abstract and therefore meaningless concept. Unless voters know who is going to be impacted by reform and how it will be paid for, it is one of those "motherhood and apple pie" ideas that means very little. For example, during the campaign, there was much emphasis, particularly from the Democratic side, on the 47 million uninsured Americans. While there is some dispute about the actual number of uninsured, it has become quite clear that the issue of the uninsured is a political loser. If 47 million Americans are uninsured, this means that over 250 million are insured, and therefore the plight of the uninsured, while a matter of vital social concern, is not an overriding daily issue for the vast majority of Americans. Although we may wish that Americans had a more altruistic, responsible attitude toward the poor and disadvantaged - perhaps along the lines of European societies - this has never been the attitude of Americans and is unlikely to change anytime soon.

So the problem remains - "what do most voters want?" The 250 million Americans who have insurance aren't that interested in universal coverage since it won't impact them directly, at least not in any positive way. What they are upset about is the cost of their own health care. With rising health insurance premiums and deductibles, Americans believe they are paying too much for health care. By and large, they are happy with the quality of care they receive, and while they might be worried about losing coverage, that is an abstract fear about the future rather than a concrete, present-day concern. Most polls bear this out, and reflect rising public unease about the direction of health care reform.

If policy makers want to address the primary concern of voters, the goal of health care reform should be to lower the real, out-of-pocket expenses of most Americans. That means lower insurance premiums and lower deductibles, without a significant rise in taxes. If health care reform could provide, say, $1,000 annually in net savings to consumers, they would probably support it, provided it didn't mean diminished quality of care, the loss of insurance or higher taxes. Maybe that's an impossible goal. If so, the policy makers need to rethink their approach to health care reform.

The bottom line? What is the average voter going to get out of all this and what will it cost? In times of economic uncertainty, most people are not going to jump on the reform applecart when it might well topple over. Why risk throwing what everyone knows is a fragile health care system off the rails, especially when the payoff for the average person is so little? Sure, we've heard the arguments that we are heading for disaster, that people are being thrown into bankruptcy daily by health care nightmares. But voters figure we don't have a disaster yet, and health care reform might just well hasten it. And while thousands of people go bankrupt, millions are merely annoyed by high costs.

Despite the ambivalence of the public, some form of health care reform is likely to pass. The question is whether it will be effectively sold to the public after it passes. The Obama administration and Congress would be wise to listen carefully to the voters, discerning their real concerns about health care and tailor legislation to those concerns. And when health care reform finally passes, in whatever form, politicians on both sides of the debate ought to continue the dialogue with the public, focusing on the issues that matter most to voters, rather than on the abstract or the ideological.

Torture Commission: A Gift to the Republican Right?

May 2009

I support a truth commission on torture. There are certainly sound moral and even political reasons to discover the truth about the outrageous abuses of the Bush era. While many people in the country -- including everyone in the White House -- would like the issue to go away, some sort of truth commission, or at least Congressional committee hearings, is probably inevitable. This is the 800-pound gorilla that is unlikely to disappear, especially with the constant drumbeat from the Republican right, and after Speaker Pelosi's less than stellar performance in her press conference this week.

But we should also be aware that the likely beneficiaries of torture hearings will be none other than the Republicans, especially those on the far right. How can that be? After all, it was the neo-cons and their conservative allies who drove the Bush administration policies that led America to a disastrous war in Iraq and lied to the public and Congress about everything from WMD's to torture policies. How could they possibly benefit from a full airing of the truth of their misdeeds?

Simple. Americans by a wide margin already hold the Bush administration and their Republican allies in Congress responsible for the terrible abuses of human rights, the Constitution and national security, not to mention the meltdown of the economy. There is almost nothing that will come out in truth commission hearings that will shock the country about the Bush crowd. If it were suddenly revealed, for example, that Dick Cheney personally gnawed off the leg of a detainee, most people would likely shrug and consider that well within the character of the former Vice President.

However, what will be an eye-opener for Americans is the news that leading Democrats were briefed on the torture policies, however obliquely, and didn't raise a fuss at the time. The fact that they knew about the torture at the time and are now protesting loudly about it, will make them appear not only complicit, but also hypocritical. Never mind the fact that the Democratic leadership had virtually no influence over the Bush administration policies. It has morphed into a case of "what did they know and when did they know it?" And we all understand where that is going. Add to the mix a heavy dose of fuel provided by Speaker Pelosi when she accused the CIA of lying to her and others in Congress about the torture program. Rest assured that the CIA will aggressively push back against that charge. Now the question becomes "who is telling the truth?" And, again, we can predict how that scenario will unfold.

Here is how the Republicans benefit from all this. First, the Republicans have nowhere to go but up. America blames them for everything from the disaster in

Iraq to the economic mess. If they manage to dirty the Democrats' previously clean hands on torture, it's a win for them. And if they can force the White House into taking sides in the debate, then it's an even bigger win, since anything President Obama says on the subject will either lose him support from the left or further alienate the right, and possibly even cost him votes in the middle of the political spectrum. While this won't derail his domestic agenda, it could distract him or slow down his efforts moving forward on the economy, health care, education and other pressing issues.

The other big win for the Republicans is that the truth commission shifts the national debate back to national security, and more specifically terrorism. This is a winning issue for the Republicans -- witness the recent presidential election when McCain, champion of national security issues, was inching ahead of Obama in the polls right before the October economic meltdown. A bright focus on terrorism is red meat for the Republicans. And if, more likely *when* there is another terrorist attack, the Republicans can expect to reap big political gains as they castigate the Democrats and White House for being "hypocritical pansies" in the war against terror.

As critical as a truth commission on torture would be for America in restoring its moral compass, we should also recognize that it will also be a gift to the Republican party, one that will keep on giving for years to come. While it is perhaps axiomatic that truth is more important than political gain, it is a bitter pill to swallow that those most responsible for the terrible abuses of the past decade are those who are most likely to benefit from an investigation into the truth.

Time to Call Off the Predators?

May 2009

No single issue that has fueled the flames of anti-Americanism in Pakistan more than the bombings of their country by our Predator drones. Since President Obama took office, there have been at least sixteen Predator strikes, which have killed about 160 people and led to widespread protests around the country. More serious than the wave of anti-Americanism is the instability that the continuing Predator strikes have brought to the fragile civilian government of President Zardari.

There is real evidence that the air strikes have done substantial damage to the leadership of Al-Qaeda and the Taliban, and they are consistent with the policy announced by President Obama during his campaign that he would take the fight to Al-Qaeda and the Taliban, even if it meant violating the territorial sovereignty of Pakistan. However, the value of the strikes may be diminishing, especially in relation to the growing anger in Pakistan which itself pushes people toward the extremists. Colonel David Kilcullen, formerly a senior adviser to General Petraeus, the US regional commander, in testimony to Congress, said "We need to call off the drones." He added that "The current path that we are on is leading us to loss of Pakistani government control over its own population." While a halt in the air assaults, even a temporary one, might give a reprieve to Al-Qaeda and the Taliban, it may be a necessary step toward stabilizing the Pakistani government.

The high-level meetings this week between President Obama, President Zardari and Afghan President Karzai represent an important challenge to all three of the leaders, and the American airstrikes are central to that challenge. Zardari must convince both Obama and Karzai that he is serious about stemming the flow of extremism inside Pakistan, and that he will have the backing in that effort from both the Pakistani military and intelligence services. Karzai must sign on to a regional solution to the crisis, and agree to the greater oversight of the funding that has been pouring into his country.

Perhaps the greatest test will be for President Obama, who will have to demonstrate not only to those in the region, but also to the American people and the rest of the world, that he can be tough in taking the battle to extremist groups like Al-Qaeda and the Taliban, and at the same time provide the political, military and economic support to governments on the front line. Finally, he needs to show the flexibility to adjust his course in midstream -- in this case, by grounding the Predators as a gesture of goodwill to the nation of Pakistan. Even though it might slow the progress we have made in damaging the leadership of Al-Qaeda and Taliban, in the long run it will prove our respect for and commitment to the Pakistani people. Because, like it or not, we are in this struggle for the long run.

Waterboarding Sean Hannity

April 2009

Sean Hannity's offer to undergo waterboarding for charity is almost too good to refuse. However, before we undertake any such extraordinary interrogation techniques (EIT's, for short) on the Fox talk show host, we should be sure to get some airtight legal opinions to make sure we won't run afoul of the Geneva Convention. I know a couple of former Justice Department employees who would fit the bill perfectly -- and I'm pretty sure they'll find a way to carve out a broad exception to the rules against torturing right-wing blowhards. If there ever was an open and shut threat to national security, Mr. Hannity fits the bill.

But what's the real purpose of waterboarding slick Sean? Is this a case of exigent circumstances? A ticking clock? "Hell, yes," as they say in neocon lingo. We need to know if Mr. Hannity really believes all the tripe he spews or is he just doing it to grab viewers and sell books? Well, actually, we already know the answer to that question without torturing the guy. But what else does he know that he's not telling us? Is there really a vast right-wing conspiracy, or is it actually a few wingnuts like Sean and Rush who are making a couple of bucks by stirring up the hackles of the left and tickling the cockles of the right? And after we get through waterboarding Sean -- 183 times sounds about right -- will we really have gotten any useful information out of him? (What do you think?)

And beyond all the legal mumbo-jumbo about international rules and conventions, would it be *morally* right to torture Sean the talk show man? Of course it would. If anyone deserves waterboarding, it is clearly Sean Hannity. In fact, he's *asking* for it. But what about the American tradition against torture? Didn't we actually prosecute Japanese officers as war criminals for waterboarding? That's true, but I'm sure there are a number of folks who would gladly face a war crimes tribunal for a chance to strip Hannity naked and subject him to simulated drowning. In the end, we have to ask whether America would be any better off for having tortured people like Mr. Hannity. And the answer to that question is -- of course we would. In fact, televising the event would probably drastically improve America's image around the world.

Which brings me to what is clearly a budding new concept in reality TV, and probably the debut of a clever marketing campaign by Fox. Look for the new series *Torture the Talk Show Host* to premiere this spring, featuring bloviators from the left and right. Picture Rush Limbaugh after a week of forced sleep deprivation. Or how about Lou Dobbs with women's underwear on his head? Or Keith Olbermann crawling on the floor with a collar around his neck? True, it may go beyond the bounds of good taste, but when did that ever slow down the onslaught of reality television? After all, the bottom line of reality TV, not to mention talk shows and cable news and much of the rest of lowest-common denominator media is (what else?) -- the bottom line. So don't preach to me about morality, folks. For a crack at Hannity on the rack, I'm almost ready to cross over to the dark side.

Investigating Bush-Cheney Torture Policies "By the Book"

April 2009

In late 1941, my grandfather, Roger Hilsman, Sr., was the US Commander of one of the southern islands of the Philippines that was attacked by the Japanese. Obeying the orders of General Douglas MacArthur, my grandfather surrendered his command and became one of thousands of Allied POWs in Asia. He survived the Bataan Death March, the transit to Japan, and harsh years in a prison camp in Northern Manchuria. Although his prison diaries do not reveal evidence of outright torture by the Japanese, the intimidation from his captors was intense, and the conditions were stark. Many men died in his camp, and, throughout Asia, Allied POWs were subjected to torture and execution in violation of the Geneva Convention, which had been first enacted by the international community in 1864, and amended to cover the treatment of prisoners of war in 1929. Fortunately, my grandfather survived his years in the prison camp, and was liberated at the end of the war by my father, a recent West Point graduate who had fought in Burma with Merrill's Marauders, been seriously wounded, and then returned to fight behind Japanese lines with the OSS.

While my grandfather was deeply scarred by his prison experience and harbored a lifelong hatred for his Japanese captors, he was able to keep in mind the distinction between those Japanese guards who had treated him honorably as a fellow soldier, and those who had treated him as something less than human. He understood, for example, that it was their job to get information from him and his fellow prisoners -- even if it was as insignificant as the location of a hidden trowel for digging vegetables. And it was his job as a soldier to deny them that information. As an American officer, my grandfather understood about rules, discipline and punishment. In fact, as the ranking officer of the prison camp, he often had to mete out harsh punishment to the Allied prisoners under his command. But, true to the spit-and-polish ethos of the American Army, whatever was done had to be "by the book."

In the world of the prison camp, both the prisoners and their Japanese captors knew exactly what "by the book" meant. The Japanese knew about the Geneva Convention, and they heard regularly from the International Red Cross, even in Northern Manchuria. Whether they choose to abide by the rules was another matter, but the rules were clear. And, as my grandfather and all the other POWs throughout Asia and elsewhere learned, some of their captors obeyed the rules, while many did not. But the rules were clear, and after the war, trials were held to punish the offenders, all according to the rule of law. Even after their grueling wartime experiences, I doubt that my grandfather or most other POWs would advocate changing the Geneva Convention, either to strengthen or loosen the protections for POWs. His view, I believe, would be to punish those who broke the rules, and exonerate the others. This is a view that is shared, in large part, by most former POWs, including Senator John McCain.

Which brings me to the current debate over the Bush-Cheney torture policies and the initial reluctance of the Obama administration to pursue investigations into the development and implementation of these policies. While it is painful and politically divisive to look back at the failures and abuses of the past, it is a necessary ingredient not only for our democracy to function, but also to implement the change that the President has championed. It would be betrayal of the sacrifices of Americans like my grandfather to selectively prosecute the low-level offenders at Abu Ghraib and ignore the policy makers who set the violations of the Geneva Convention in motion. While I am not personally convinced by the legalistic exceptions to the Geneva Conventions that distinguish "detainees" captured during the invasion of Afghanistan from "prisoners of war," or the "exigent circumstances" argument that the Bush administration used to justify torture, perhaps there need to be exceptions carved into the Conventions. However, this will only get done if nations honestly investigate and prosecute violations.

I understand that this is not a top priority for the Obama White House, nor should it be. There are many more pressing problems at their doorstep, beginning with the economy, health care reform, the energy crisis and global warming, to name a few. Revisiting the torture policies of the Bush era should be the least of their concerns. But the White House should not stand in the way of legitimate investigations of violations of American or international law. It is the responsibility of the Justice Department -- free of political consideration -- to investigate and determine whether laws have been violated, and by whom. This may be a dirty job and it may take a long time, but it has to be done. And it must be done, as my grandfather would say, "by the book."

Madoff, AIG and the American Gospel of Success

March 2009

New York Times columnist David Brooks recently wrote about the American gospel of success, which encourages "middle-class people to strive, risk and make money." The economic downturn has caused a brief lull in the relentless American success drive, writes Brooks, "But if there is one thing we can be sure of, this pause will not last. The cultural DNA of the past 400 years will not be erased. The pendulum will swing hard. The gospel of success will recapture the imagination."

Maybe. But it is also worth considering that the American people may have learned a sobering, valuable lesson: that the overpowering drive for money and success that has been a driving force in American culture (at least for the past 200 years since the dawn of the Industrial Revolution) may have been sorely tempered by the excesses of the past three decades. Unrestrained striving for money and success may have made sense in a world of unlimited resources and opportunities, but on an increasingly crowded, polluted and interdependent planet, the human race may not be able to indulge the "cultural DNA" of a society that has Darwinian opportunism as a credo.

Does this mean we have to throw in the towel? Admit that the future looks bleak with no hope for improvement? Hardly. Throughout our history, Americans have been both proud of and admired for an even more important cultural trait -- our unbridled optimism. What brought the Puritans to America was not the drive for money or success, but a hope for a better life for themselves and their children. Wave after wave of immigrants that have come to America are not lured by the "gospel of success" but the opportunity for greater freedom, equality and hope. Certainly, material comforts are an important part of a happy life, but most Americans also count community, family and security as equally key components of the American dream.

Somewhere along the line, our optimism and enthusiasm became confused with ambition and even greed. Our dreams for a better life were translated into "Dream and grow rich." In his column, Brooks quotes the late nineteenth century Baptist minister Russell Cowell, who traveled the country preaching the gospel of wealth: "I say that you ought to get rich, and it is your duty to get rich ... Money is power, and you ought to be reasonably ambitious to have it. You ought, because you can do more good with it than you could without it." Can we really say, after the Madoff scandal, the AIG bonuses and all the excesses of the past decades that we can do more good with wealth than without it? Experience suggests that the opposite is the case -- that men do more evil with wealth than good.

Even before the financial meltdown, Americans had begun to turn away from the blind "gospel of success." Barack Obama's message of hope was tempered by a heavy dose of reality. "Yes, we can" did not mean "Yes, we can become rich and powerful" or "Yes, we can dictate our values and way of life to the rest of humanity." Obama's message was that we can restore the core American values of common sense, community, pride and, yes, a sense of energetic optimism. In the fields of health care, education, environmental protection and other critical issues, Obama was not saying that we want to be "the greatest on earth," but rather that we ought to have health care and educational systems that reinforce our core values of equality and opportunity. In foreign affairs, he has adopted the view of partnering with the rest of the world, rather than striving to impose our values or our superior power on other nations.

While conservatives may argue that greed and self-interest will ultimately be restored and that the social Darwinism of the free market will triumph, most Americans are more optimistic. Call us cockeyed optimists, but those of us who embraced the message of hope over the past year believe in a more temperate future for America. We believe in a free market, but also in a level playing field. We believe in capitalism, but with a referee. And we believe that the core American values of equality, opportunity and fairness will always trump greed, ambition and self-interest.

Putting the Heart into Economic Stimulus

February 2009

At a town hall event this week in Fort Myers, Florida, President Obama took an important step down the road to economic recovery. No, it wasn't a policy proposal that he made, or a thoughtful answer to a citizen's question, or even the announcement that his stimulus package had passed in the Senate. It was when he climbed down from the speaker's platform to comfort Henrietta Hughes.

After telling the president that she was "praying for him," Hughes explained that she and her son were living in their small car, moving around the county each night and using showers in the parks. "I am in urgent need now. Please help," she pleaded. Obama's response was swift and appropriate - he climbed down from his high perch to give her a hug.

While it is easy to be cynical about emotional gestures by politicians, Obama's spontaneous expression of concern should be a wakeup call to those on all sides of the debate over the economic stimulus package. As we argue over too much or too little money, too soon or too late, there is a tidal wave of suffering that is building daily in our nation and will very shortly be crashing down upon us.

The human suffering is not about securities derivatives, or bad banks, or Keynesian economics. It is about our cousin who works in construction, or our friend from high school who sells insurance, or our nephew who is in college. It is about our neighbors who are facing foreclosure but are ashamed to tell us, our co-worker who has just been laid off, our barber with a sick child. It is our friends and neighbors, our brothers and sisters, our parents and grandparents, our children.

As the President has said, "We've had a good debate, now it is time to act." Of course, it is important to embrace bipartisanship, to be fiscally responsible, to punish wrongdoers and not to reward moral laxity. But if we meet a man walking down a road, already thin and gaunt from hunger, do we ask whether he needs 1,000 calories to survive instead of 1,500? Do we speculate whether he might live another week or so without food before we feed him? No. We give him food. Now.

Amidst all the wrangling over the policy intricacies of economic stimulus, something very important is getting lost in the debate -- our hearts. We are confronted not only with the prospect of suffering, but its reality. Food banks are being swamped with new clients, many of whom are there for the first time. These are not anybodies. They are our friends, our neighbors, our parents, our grandparents, our children. They are Henrietta Hughes and so many more like her.

We should all understand that there is no choice other than acting quickly to stimulate the economy. The stakes are higher than any we have known in most of our lifetimes. Whether it is $800 billion or a trillion doesn't really matter. What matters is that we take action. If Americans understand the choice they are facing - to feed a starving man rather than debate how many calories he needs or how much longer he can go without food - they will make the right choice. And Americans will also come to understand that it was wrong to waste too much valuable time quibbling about calories or timing, especially if the starving man dies.

Economic Stimulus: Fixing the Car While We're Driving It

February 2009

A silver lining amidst the dark clouds of financial gloom may be the unique opportunity to remake our economy in a way that provides opportunities for all Americans, not just the privileged few. The Hope Street Group, a bipartisan, volunteer policy organization dedicated to building an Opportunity Economy, believes that the financial meltdown offers just such a challenge.

The Hope Street Group, founded a few years ago by a core group of young businesspeople, academics and professionals, promotes the general notion that investing in human capital is the best way to build our economy for the future, and has offered specific policy proposals in areas like healthcare, education, corporate welfare and housing. The group - of which I am a member, along with several thousand others around the country - has also developed an Economic Opportunity Index, which is a valuable tool for measuring economic opportunity in our complex society.

This week, the Executive Director of the Hope Street Group, Monique Nadeau, made an interesting point about the economic stimulus package. "We know how critical it is to address the short term crisis," said Nadeau, "But if we don't start at the same time to strengthen the true drivers of economic opportunity, we risk bouncing from crisis to crisis. We're in the unfortunate position of having to fix the car while we're driving it."

Nadeau's argument is that we can't lose sight of the forest for the trees (or the trees for the forest), and that the package should focus not only on the immediate crisis, but also on the long-term goals and standards of funding in health care, education, housing and other economic opportunity drivers. Beyond the immediate impact of the economic stimulus, are we building a productive foundation for future economic growth? While Republicans and centrist Democrats have raised some of these issues in discussing the various stimulus plans, this is truly a concern that should cross both partisan and ideological divides.

The challenge of "fixing a car while we're driving it" is to make sure that we don't let the economy crash, while at the same time making the fundamental repairs necessary to keep it running well into the future. And while there is no good reason to delay passage of an economic stimulus package -- which would send the economy into a ditch -- we need to make room in the package has the kind of long-term reconstructive features that will lead to jobs and other kinds of economic opportunities for all Americans well into the future.

After all, what the economic stimulus package is really about is salvaging the American Dream for all Americans. Only by taking a long-term view of economic growth and opportunity, even as we meet the short-term crisis, will we be able to restore that Dream.

Is It Time for "Job Bonds?"

February 2009

During World War II, Americans were encouraged to buy "war bonds" to support the war effort. From Hollywood to Madison Avenue to Main Street there were bond drives that stressed our patriotic duty to invest in victory by buying US Savings Bonds. By the end of the war, nearly half of all Americans had bought war bonds, raising nearly $185 billion -- a staggering sum at the time -- to support the troops.

As we face another global crisis, maybe it's time to invest in victory over the financial crisis with bonds to create jobs -- call them "job bonds." The idea would be a pretty simple corollary to President Obama's economic stimulus plan, which would dedicate over $800 billion to infrastructure spending and other projects that would create jobs right away.

The "job bonds" would have a similar purpose , but would be funded by the investment of all Americans in our future, and wouldn't cost taxpayers a penny. These bonds could also be targeted toward specific spending areas. For example, you could buy a bond that would pay for green technology projects, or for improving our bridges and highways. And the bonds would be just like the old war bonds, paying a decent interest rate and backed by the government.

For the ninety percent of Americans who still have jobs, and for those who have a little extra to invest in our country, wouldn't it make sense to buy a few "job bonds" rather than let the money sit in a savings account or CD at some bank holding company with overpaid executives living on government bailouts? A number of states and several foreign countries have already either proposed or offered "economic stimulus bonds," which would be sold to investors and dedicated to providing local economies with a much-needed jumpstart.

I'm not an economist, and there are probably a hundred technical reasons why "job bonds" are a lousy idea. For one thing, they don't get consumers spending again on big-screen TV's or flashy cars. But I don't see that many people out on spending sprees lately. So why not put our money to work creating jobs with long-overdue infrastructure improvements rather than give it to the banks to invest in securities derivatives that don't create anything of value?

The idea of "job bonds" wouldn't be to replace the economic stimulus package. We need government intervention immediately to stop a global economic freefall. But why not give individual Americans a chance to make a meaningful investment in our country's recovery? If nothing else, buying a "job bond" would be a lot more satisfying than going shopping for something we may not even need.

After 9/11 and the invasion of Iraq, George Bush suggested that Americans could support the country by "going shopping," which struck a lot of the public as a strange way to show our wartime patriotism. In the face of global financial meltdown, when many workers are facing the loss of jobs and when most Americans are reluctant to do a lot of shopping, "job bonds" might be a more creative and constructive way to help our country in this time of crisis.

Obama or FDR: Whose Strategy Will Work Better?

January 2009

Jonathan Alter's engaging and often startling book about the first hundred days of Franklin Roosevelt's presidency, *The Defining Moment*, is chock full of parallels to Barack Obama's transition and possibly Obama's first hundred days. The obvious similarity is the deep economic crisis that faced Roosevelt and now confronts Obama. Both were elected, in large part, because of the public's fear of economic collapse and their repudiation of the policies of the outgoing Republican administrations.

Herbert Hoover had been slow to act in response to the 1929 Crash, insisting on pursuing a *laissez-faire*, free market approach to the crisis when most economists had realized that those policies would only worsen the crisis. George Bush, while he was quicker to act when confronted with the dangers of the downturn, was not only slow to recognize the seriousness of the overheated housing market, but also was complicit, along with his fellow Republicans, in the lax oversight of financial institutions and markets.

One significant difference between the Roosevelt transition and that of Barack Obama is the swiftness with which the Obama transition team has moved to address the nation's economic crisis. After the November, 1932 election, when the economic downturn was already in full force and the nation was faced with widespread bank closing, FDR refused to take an active role in economic policy until the day of his inauguration in March, 1933. (The inauguration occurred in March until it was later changed to January, partly because of the lengthy FDR interregnum).

While Hoover dithered with free market solutions, occasionally reaching out half-heartedly to FDR, President-elect Roosevelt refused to take a strong stand, or even send specific signals about what actions he might take. In fact, on the night before the inauguration, Hoover was still negotiating with Roosevelt, who had assiduously avoided most of his entreaties, for a joint statement on a "bank holiday," which would give banks across the nation a breather from relentless depositor demands.

On the day of his inauguration, FDR finally revealed his hand, dramatically announcing a nationwide bank holiday that was almost joyously received by both the banks and the American public, and which initiated a fervid hundred days of legislation, proclamations and executive actions to address the crisis. Historian Alter believes that the cagey Roosevelt carefully hid his hand until Inauguration Day -- as the economy sank deeper into crisis -- in order to have the maximum impact during his first hundred days.

Alter argues that if the crisis had been less severe, or if FDR had revealed his plans earlier, there would have been time for opposition to his plans to crystallize on Capitol Hill and in the public mind. By waiting until he was sworn in to unveil his prescription for the crisis, FDR succeeded in neutralizing any opposition and swiftly enacting most of his policies. While it may be seen as a cynical move, Alter makes the case that it ultimately bolstered FDR's effectiveness.

Obama has taken a different tack by coming out swinging early with his proposals and seizing the initiative even before he has been sworn in. Certainly there are significant differences between both the economic and political situation in 1933 and 2009 that are guiding the strategy of the Obama transition. And while there are some signs that opposition is developing on Capitol Hill and in some segments of the public to his $825 billion rescue package, the Obama team seems to be betting that an early attack on the problem will not only prove to be the most effective strategy, but will also lessen the economic turmoil and suffering. The next hundred days will likely establish whether the FDR strategy or the Obama strategy will work better.

Why Barack Obama Needs to Fail

January 2009

Early in his campaign, Barack Obama said "I'm human and I'm going to make mistakes." But as the election campaign wore on and Obama racked up impressive victories first in the primaries and then in the general election, there was a growing feeling among his supporters and even some in the press that he could do no wrong. Obama himself joked about this at the traditional Al Smith dinner when he said, "Contrary to rumors you may have heard, I was not born in a manger."

The minor stumbles of the past few weeks, from the invitation of Rick Warren to speak at the inauguration, to the slow response to the Blagojevich scandal, to the bungled nominating process of Leon Panetta, have proven that Obama is indeed human, prone to mistakes like all the rest of us. As insignificant as these early failures have been, they are important milestones which Obama must cross to govern effectively.

Remember for a moment the disasters wrought by the Bush administration, from the invasion and conduct of the war in Iraq to the bungling of Hurricane Katrina relief to the heinous lack of oversight of the financial industry. All of these were brought about by a single-minded determination to avoid failure - or at least the appearance of failure. "Failure is not an option" could easily have been the slogan of the Bush years, a credo that ultimately led to fiasco after fiasco.

Not only is failure an option, it is an imperative. Leaders who actively seek to avoid failure are destined to choose the most expedient, and therefore the most treacherous path. Only by embracing failure can we test our mettle as a country and finally succeed in our goals. If we are afraid to fail, we will simply become mired in the status quo, following over and over again a path that leads nowhere.

When Franklin Roosevelt said that "We have nothing to fear but fear itself," he was speaking most specifically about our fear of failure. Again and again, FDR tackled the challenge of a struggling economy and a staggering political system, trying out new programs and then quickly jettisoning them when they failed. Without its many failures, Roosevelt's New Deal would never have become a success.

Obama also needs to fail to strengthen his political mandate. Through his mistakes and missteps, he can establish the depth and breadth of his support. If his supporters on the left abandon him over his centrist positions on social issues or the economy, or if the right wing is able to capitalize on his failure to swiftly end the fiscal crisis, then his mandate will fade, perhaps quickly. But if he can steer a course that alienates only some of his core supporters, while drawing in the mainstream of the country to his vision of change, he will have built the foundation for success.

For too long, Americans have been fed the "win at any cost" mantra, which divides the world into winners and losers, and ignores our responsibility to our communities, our nation and our planet. It is time for us to change that credo, and we can begin by acknowledging that mistakes are not only human, but they are also critical ingredients to success. And we also should remember that both the failures and the successes do not belong to Barack Obama, or any other one individual, but to all of us.

The Bush Presidency: Shakespearean Tragedy or Cruel Farce?

December 2008

As the Bush era draws to a tragicomic close -- with shoes being hurled at the American president -- it might be tempting to portray the Bush presidency in Shakespearean terms, as a tale of overarching arrogance and hubris that led to his ultimate downfall. In fact, the presidency of George Bush hardly fits the bill. Bush himself described his disastrous tenure as "joyous" and there is barely a hint of personal tragedy or even discomfort in his legacy. Most telling was Bush's response to the shoe-throwing incident, when he wondered out loud what the fellow's "cause" might be, ignoring the widespread death and destruction visited on the Iraq people in the wake of the American invasion.

Unlike earlier failed presidents like Herbert Hoover and Richard Nixon, Bush does not seem to acknowledge or even recognize the destruction that he has wrought. At the end of their presidencies, Hoover and Nixon were tortured individuals, trying in vain to redeem themselves from the scorn of history. Despite their obvious suffering, or perhaps because of it, this cast Hoover and Nixon as characters in an overarching tragedy on a grand scale. There is no such grandeur in the Bush exit, even though the damage and suffering that he caused is arguably greater than either Hoover or Nixon.

In part, this may because Hoover and Nixon were, in many ways, gifted and talented individuals who were undone by their own tragic flaws. In Hoover's case, it was his deep-seated belief in capitalism, while in Nixon's case, it was his own myopia and paranoia in the exercise of power. Bush, on the other hand, brought few gifts to the White House beyond aw-shucks mannerisms and powerful friends. His commitment to spreading freedom -- and even to his own religious principles -- seem in retrospect to have been convenient *ex post facto* rationales for his political strategems.

What is most breathtaking about the Bush presidency -- beyond its arrogance and aggressive bluster -- is the sheer incompetence and lack of vision that was endemic to the administration. A more profound misreading of the state of the world and of the global balance of power could hardly be imagined, from the incoherent, unfocused declaration of a "global war on terror," to the unprecedented, preemptive invasion of a sovereign nation and the almost criminally benign neglect of overheated financial markets. The use of torture is but one particularly repugnant example of not only the Bush administration's moral bankruptcy, but also of their sheer incompetency. While countries like Israel, England and

Germany - no strangers to terrorist tactics -- had long since developed much more sophisticated, and less morally offensive, interrogation techniques, the Bush administration applied outmoded, ineffective and immoral tactics that did not, and could not, achieve results.

At the center of all this was the blindly affable Bush, profoundly and blissfully ignorant of the fiasco over which he was presiding. While a special place in outer darkness must be reserved for his own monumental failures, the blame must be shared. The first circle is clearly those policy makers who, for the sake of infamy, must be mentioned by name: Dick Cheney, Donald Rumsfeld, Condeleezza Rice, Richard Perle, Paul Wolfowitz, Douglas Feith, George Tenet and Paul Bremer. Although perhaps not personally as culpable, though clearly complicitous, were Colin Powell, who could have taken the courageous path of resignation, or General Tommy Franks, who must have seen the folly of the Iraq invasion, yet was a key enabler.

The responsibility, unfortunately, doesn't end there. Too many members of Congress - both Republicans and Democrats - put their heads down and their hands up, voting for a preemptive war that was impulsive and misguided, and then never did enough to stop the ongoing fiasco. And, finally, some blame has to rest with the American people. Those who supported the war must bear responsibility for condoning a destructive and misguided course, while those who opposed it must take responsibility for not doing enough to stop the madness in its tracks.

Sadly, much of the same incompetent stewardship that was the hallmark of the Iraq war was at work in other arenas, from Katrina to the economy, as we have discovered to our dismay over the past six months. While the Bush administration and the Republican do-nothing attitude towards regulating corporate fraud may be only partly to blame for our current dire economic straits, it is clear that they were not even bothering to rearrange the deck chairs as this Titanic began to sink. Ultimately, however, the American people must do some real soul-searching in the wake of a Presidency that was profoundly destructive of much that is good about America. The tragedy is hardly Shakespearean - characters like Bush, Cheney and the rest don't merit that kind of prominence. But it is a tragedy nonetheless - for us as individuals and a nation. A tragedy that will take a long time to overcome, and that has surely rocked us to our souls.

Do We Need the Republican Party?

December 2008

As a lifelong Democrat (my father worked for JFK) and a recent Democratic Congressional candidate, I have spent my life working to beat the pants off Republicans. And as a citizen who has suffered through the abuses of the Bush administration and the Republican rubber-stamp Congress, I would like nothing more than to see the architects of the last eight disastrous years banished to the far reaches of outer darkness.

However, if the Republican party were truly to disappear as a national political force (a fate they themselves wished on the Democrats), the nation would actually be worse off for it. By the way, this seems to be exactly what the current leadership of the Republican party has in mind. For the past eight years, the conservative wing of the GOP -- who are currently at the helm of the party - have steered a course straight for the rocks, alienating nearly every segment of the country except for the most reactionary elements of conservative America. From Latinos to big business, from Reagan Democrats to suburban moms, GOP leaders have waged war against the mainstream of our country, and they are now getting the full blowback of that ill-conceived and unjustified war.

So why not let the Republican party, now in the hands of a disgraced and disreputable conservative minority, head straight for the dustbin of history, where much of America now believes it belongs? Shouldn't there be some consequences for their recklessness and irresponsibility? From a moral standpoint, absolutely. But from a practical standpoint, we still need a responsible - and I emphasize the word "responsible" - opposition party.

The past few months of the financial crisis demonstrate the dangers of a renegade and irresponsible opposition. While the Republican leadership might have been expected to navigate a compromise in Congress with the help of the White House, the Democrats in Congress and President-elect Obama, instead they resorted to their old stonewalling tactics, determined to sabotage any constructive, bipartisan action. In the name of a rigid and outmoded ideology, they went back to the barricades when the rest of the country was trying to muddle through this mess together. The result--the GOP further alienated mainstream America.

Not that there are not a few voices within the party who have tried to be responsible. Even Bob Corker, who ultimately came down on the side of the know-nothings, tried to make a responsible argument against the auto bailout before he was drowned out by the voices of the Republican stonewallers. And there are other examples of moderate Republicans who could make important contributions to a national debate aimed at practical solutions, if they weren't swamped by the forces of extremism in their own party.

Ironically, the Republicans will have a real opportunity during the early days of the Obama administration to stake out reasonable opposing positions that might offer to restore a least of modicum of their vanished credibility with the American public. And responsible voices of opposition would likely be welcomed by the Obama White House, as they always are in times of crisis. After all, Barack Obama has promised not only change, but also a new approach to leadership that bridges historic partisan divides. When will the Republicans - both moderates and reasonable conservatives - push back against the extremist elements in their own party? It would not only be good for the GOP - possibly rescuing it from oblivion - but it might even (gasp!) be good for the country.

Hi, My Name is America and I'm a Credit Addict

December 2008

In light of all the six-step, eight-step and ten-step proposals floating around Washington, I thought I'd offer the following twelve-step program for recovery from the financial crisis:

1. Admitted that we were powerless over our addiction to credit, leverage, derivative swaps and cheap gadgets from China, and that our lives have become unmanageable, not to mention uncreditworthy.
2. Came to believe that a higher power in the form of God, the heads of the central banks or possibly Barack Obama, could restore us to sanity.
3. Made a decision to turn our will and our lives over to the care of God, the central bank chiefs or possibly Barack Obama, not necessarily in that order.
4. Made a searching and fearless moral inventory of ourselves, our credit card statements, our 401(k)'s, our mortgage balances, our house values, and our Christmas list.
5. Admitted to God, to ourselves, and to another human being (beginning with our spouses) the exact nature of our spending on lattes at Starbucks, flat-screen TVs, Ipods and trips to the Bahamas.
6. Were entirely ready to have God, the central bank chiefs or possibly Barack Obama remove all these defects of character (provided we can still keep our houses, jobs and cars)
7. Humbly asked any of the above to remove our shortcomings and also forgive us our debts, particularly the $397 we are still paying for that household espresso machine that we never used.
8. Made a list of all persons we had harmed, and became willing to make amends to them all, except of course for the loan officer we cursed out over the phone and the appraiser who said our house was worth approximately seven times its actual value.
9. Made direct amends to such people wherever possible, except when to do so would injure them or others, especially since it would be useless to apologize to our former boss who we punched out when he laid us off with two hours notice because he's now unemployed himself.
10. Continued to take personal inventory and when we were wrong promptly admitted it, especially when we inadvertently told our wife that her IRA is up 25% when it is actually down 125%.
11. Sought through prayer, meditation, whining, begging and pleading to improve our conscious contact with God, the chiefs of the central banks and possibly Barack Obama, praying only for knowledge of Their Will for us and the power to carry that out, with the divine intervention of Chairman Barney Frank and Treasury

Secretary Hank Paulson.

12. Having had a spiritual awakening -- not to mention a rude financial shock -- as the result of these steps, we tried to carry this message to other credit addicts everywhere and to practice these principles in all our affairs, or at least until the next time a financial bubble comes along.

The Auto Bailout and Post-Partisanship

December 2008

I was shocked to find myself agreeing with Republican Senator Bob Corker as he questioned the Detroit automakers last week -- at least with his assessment of the problem, if not his conclusions. Corker put it in stark terms -- we wouldn't be in this particular mess if it weren't for General Motors, which is likely to go bankrupt by the end of the month without a federal bailout. Ford, on the other hand, borrowed billions of dollars last year at low rates and, if not exactly sitting pretty, is at least like to survive into next year. And Chrysler, the third leg of this dysfunctional troika, is owned by a private holding company, which is loaded with cash but reluctant to put another nickel into what is clearly the weakest link in a failing industry. The real shock is that the automakers, and other members of the Senate committee, pretty much agreed with the picture Corker painted.

The question, of course, is what can be done about this mess? Everybody in the auto industry is staring into the abyss -- the automakers, the unions, the suppliers, the dealers -- not to mention the government and the taxpayers. There's plenty of blame to go around -- including Hank Paulson and the Treasury Department for refusing to release a few billion in TARP funds to the auto industry while the banks are taking hundreds of billions in public money to pay dividends and make acquisitions. And Ron Gettelfinger brought up the excellent point that American trade policies which permitted countries like South Korea to export tens of thousands of cars to the U.S. while at the same time severely restricting imports of American vehicles. Unfortunately, issues of free trade and industrial policy get tabled while the government deals with the potential bankruptcy of our entire auto industry.

Dr. Mark Zandi, the chief economist for Moody's Economy.com, presented what is likely to be the shape of the eventual compromise. Zandi argued for an immediate $17 billion to go to GM and Chrysler (with nothing to Ford) and a strict set of benchmarks to be revisited by the end of March, when he predicted that the automakers would be coming back for more money. The eventual price tag for saving Detroit, Zandi estimated, could reach $75-$125 billion. Although he didn't say so, it sounded like Zandi was implicitly agreeing with Corker's assessment of the predicament, but wasn't willing to let the automakers fail in the midst of this crisis, since it could launch the economy into an even more serious meltdown. Zandi's compromise proposal, of course, raises the question whether this kind of halfway measure will ever work, or whether it is the beginning of a slippery slope, pouring good money after bad. In effect, that is the crux of Corker's argument.

What this latest iteration of the economic meltdown suggests is that we ought to be looking at the larger issues raised by the crisis in the American economy - indeed in global capitalism itself. Do we need big changes in our economic structure, or would that be overreacting to the present crisis? If we need big changes, do we need to make those changes immediately, or can the fundamental change be more incremental? Ultimately, how much control do we have over the fast-moving crisis? This last may not be a rhetorical question, since we may have more control than we think, once we figure out more clearly what the challenges are that we face.

Which brings me back to my shock at agreeing with Republican Senator Bob Corker's observations, if not his conclusions. Although Corker undeniably comes from a very different political and ideological perspective than I do, and his conclusions about what actions should be taken are also very different from mine, there is no denying that his assessment of the problem is dead on. This is the kind of honest, concrete discussion that has been missing for the past eight years of a Republican administration. It also bodes well for a forthright dialogue on our economic woes. I would expect that President-elect Obama will be equally blunt in his assessment of the scope and nature of the challenges, and will engage the American people and Congress in a refreshingly honest dialogue on the way forward. In the midst a very dire crisis, that is one hopeful sign.

Twilight, Britney Spears and Grand Theft Auto: The Key to Obama's Foreign Policy?

December 2008

One of the biggest legacies of the Bush administration is America's tattered global image. Karen Hughes, Bush's longtime confidante, realized (too late!) that America had a public relations problem and began to wage "a war of ideas," which mostly meant lecturing the rest of the world about freedom and democracy. The net result: anti-American sentiment at historic highs while Islamic fundamentalism flourished. As former UN Ambassador Richard Holbrooke pointedly asked "How can a man in a cave out-communicate the world's leading communications society?"

While most of America's image problem was due to the disastrous Bush foreign policy, it was also the result of America's failure both to craft a compelling message and to deliver that message effectively. In other words, the failure to tell a convincing story. Both the strategy (message content) and tactics (message delivery) of what is called "public diplomacy" have failed miserably in the past eight years, and even before.

Instead of showcasing the creativity, diversity and openness of American society, we have been arrogantly lecturing the rest of humanity about freedom and democracy. In a world where millions of people are enamored of our movies, music and technology, we try to engage them in a "battle of ideas" over arcane theories of government. All the while, we ignore some of the most powerful communications and technology platforms in history -- from new ways of storytelling to social networking on the internet -- in favor of old-fashioned messaging that is more 19th century than 21st century.

Like it or not, pop culture and technology are among our most valuable exports and most identifiable brand. People may not be interested in American-style democracy, but they avidly consume our movies, music, fashion and technology to the tune of a $100 billion a year. There may be a lot more to America than our pop culture or technology, but why ignore these powerful products of our vibrant and open culture, and focus instead on the almost sternly puritanical vision of America?

Especially when our pop culture and technology are so effective in communicating with the rest of the world? Certainly the substance of American foreign policy -- the strident militancy and arrogance of the Bush years -- will have to change before we can restore America's tattered image. But we shouldn't ignore the medium of pop culture and technology -- the hit movie _Twilight_, teen idol Britney Spears and video game sensation *Grand Theft Auto* -- in communicating our message to the world.

So how should the Obama administration institute Public Diplomacy 2.0? First, create a central agency like FDR's Office of War Information (later the US Information Agency) to oversee the public diplomacy efforts of all government departments, including State, Defense, CIA, AID and others.

Secondly, enlist the private sector as a partner in public diplomacy. Get the best talent from media, entertainment and technology. The government needs help. It doesn't have the resources, experience or expertise to go it alone.

Thirdly, set achievable, measureable goals. Public diplomacy initiatives in the past failed because they had no clearly defined goals and no measurable results. Public diplomacy, like any other messaging or branding effort, should be expected to produce definable, quantifiable results.

Finally, employ the most up-to-date communications strategies and technologies. Much of America's public diplomacy effort has been backward and tradition-bound, virtually ignoring a host of new techniques and technologies.

All around the world, people still admire America for its energy, creativity, openness and diversity. But since 9/11, our public diplomacy has focused more on our ideology than on our image, and is failing in the battle of ideas. As we embrace a combination of military might and diplomatic persuasion in our dealings with the rest of the world -- the "soft power" approach that President-elect Obama has embraced -- we must also recognize the pressing need for change in the way we craft and deliver America's message to the world.

www.ingramcontent.com/pod-product-compliance
Lightning Source LLC
Chambersburg PA
CBHW050451290526
45786CB00006B/2242